"[Erin Brigham helps] s ₁₁₅ not only bridge insights from the Catholic tradition with contemporary justice issues but also reexamine their perceptions and convictions in light of community encounters. Her treatment of Catholic social theory and praxis remains accessible without sacrificing depth. The embedded reflection questions will support educators as they navigate this demanding yet indispensable pedagogy."

—Kristin E. Heyer
Bernard J. Hanley Chair in Religious Studies
Santa Clara University

"Erin Brigham provides an accessible introduction to the riches of the Catholic social tradition for twenty-first-century students. . . . The reflection questions, summaries, and vignettes in each chapter situate Catholic social teaching as a living tradition . . . [and encourage students] to reflect upon the assumptions and values that influence their interpretations of social issues and their practices of responsible action."

—Jennifer Reed-Bouley
College of Saint Mary, Omaha, NE

"Erin Brigham's *See, Judge, Act* . . . applies key principles in Catholic social thought . . . to contemporary concerns. Vignettes show how students grapple with racism and white privilege, immigration, unemployment, living wage and workers, rights, poverty and economic justice, war and peace making, climate change, environmental racism, and other issues in service activities."

—Lois Ann Lorentzen
Professor, Theology and Religious Studies, and Co-Director,
The Center for Latino/a Studies in the Americas
at the University of San Francisco

Created by the publishing team of Anselm Academic.

Cover image: © AP Photo / The Joplin Globe, T. Rob Brown
Steve Willey, co-owner of Willey Construction of Joplin, Mo., works with his crew to install trusses over the Volunteer House Friday morning, Jan. 20, 2012, in the Joplin tornado zone near the intersection of 25th Street and Joplin Avenue. The Volunteer House has been signed by many hundreds of volunteers who have helped with Joplin's recovery. The city of Joplin plans to move the house and make a memorial out of it.

Printed in the United States of America

7048

ISBN 978-1-59982-154-2, Print

Author Acknowledgments

Many talented and generous people contributed to this book. I would like to thank Maura Hagarty, managing editor at Anselm Academic, whose patient and insightful guidance made this book possible. I am incredibly grateful to Jennifer Reed-Bouley for her careful review of the book. Jennifer's dedication to her students and her passion for Catholic social teaching contributed a number of improvements to this text.

I would also like to thank supportive and inspiring colleagues at the University of San Francisco (USF), particularly Mike Duffy, Director of the Joan and Ralph Lane Center for Catholic Studies and Social Thought. I have been blessed with exceptional department chairs who have supported my professional development and mentored me in my teaching and writing, especially Lois Lorentzen and Vincent Pizzuto. I am most grateful for the many USF faculty who motivated me in the Thursday writing group over the past couple of years.

Like many faculty members, I started teaching a service-learning course with great intentions but with little knowledge about how to make service learning successful. I have been fortunate to learn from dedicated community partners, especially the Faithful Fools Street Ministry and Quesada Gardens. I have also relied on the resources of USF's Leo T. McCarthy Center for Public Service and the Common Good. Julie Reed, Star Moore, Andrea Wise, and the student Advocates for Community Engagement have influenced my approach to service learning and have helped me work through a number of service-learning dilemmas over the years.

I would also like to thank my students of Catholic social thought, who have taught me the most about the value of service learning. I have watched students begin the class with a fear of leaving campus and finish the semester with a real appreciation for one of the overlooked communities in San Francisco—communities that tourists often miss but that bring so much life to this great city. It is truly a privilege to witness the transformative potential of education.

Finally, I want to thank my husband, Dana Wolfe. Every challenge is easier and every accomplishment is sweeter since I found a great partner.

Publisher Acknowledgments

Thank you to Jennifer Reed-Bouley of the College of Saint Mary, Omaha, Nebraska, for reviewing this work in progress.

See, Judge, Act

Catholic Social Teaching and Service Learning

Erin M. Brigham

CONTENTS

INTRODUCTION

The main title of this text repeats a phrase—*see–judge–act*—that is associated with Belgian Catholic priest Joseph Cardijn who worked with lay Catholics to connect their faith with social action. During the post–World War I era, an era marked by economic depression, Cardijn reached out to young working-class Catholics by founding the Young Christian Workers (YCW) in 1924.[1] The organization provided a place for laypeople to relate their struggles for justice in the workplace to an emerging tradition of Catholic social thought.[2] Cardijn introduced the process of seeing, judging, and acting in meetings of the YCW to encourage people to observe situations, to evaluate them based on the Gospels, and to act in ways that respond to observed injustices. The YCW was just one of a number of Catholic associations that mobilized laypeople to address social issues during this era. Others include the Catholic Worker movement founded by Dorothy Day and Peter Maurin and Friendship House established by Catherine De Hueck.[3] As the young people involved in the YCW moved on to new phases of life, new types of movements emerged. For example, in 1949, Pat and Patty Crowley founded the Christian Family Movement, which went beyond the earlier movements by encouraging Catholics and adherents of other religions to work together to bring about social justice for families.[4] Cardijn's use of the see-judge-act process with the YCW highlights an important aspect of the Catholic social tradition: everyone—lay and ordained—shares responsibility for social analysis and action.

---

1. Joseph Willke, "The Worker-Priest Experiment in France," *America* (April, 1984): 253.

2. Ibid.

3. See Marvin Mich, *Catholic Social Teaching and Movements* (New London, CT: Twenty-Third Publications, 1998), 62–72.

4. Ibid., 72.

Though the phrase *see-judge-act* emerged in a Catholic context, it describes a process that people use implicitly and explicitly in many different contexts to observe situations, to evaluate them in light of understandings of what is good and right, and to act in ways to improve the situation. History is full of examples of inspiring people who model this process. Civil rights leader Martin Luther King Jr. observed the social injustices perpetuated by racism in the United States, drew on his faith and values to denounce racism as morally wrong, and acted out of his convictions to advocate for racial justice. Nobel Peace Prize recipient Mother Teresa saw the suffering caused by poverty on the streets of Calcutta, reflected on the situation in light of teachings of the Gospels, and responded with compassionate service. Also, consider the college student who observes educational inequalities in her city, evaluates the situation based on her conviction that everyone should have the opportunity to receive a good education and decides to tutor low-income youth on a regular basis.

This book provides an introduction to both the Catholic social tradition and the process of seeing, judging, and acting. It is designed especially for service-learning courses that invite students to *see* social situations, *judge* them in light of principles drawn from the Catholic Church's social teaching and from their own values and beliefs, and *act* in response to observed injustices. This introduction will provide an overview of the three steps or stages of the see-judge-act process, discuss the use of the process in conjunction with service learning, and explore the relationship between the process and the Catholic social tradition.

The See-Judge-Act Process

See: Social Analysis

Seeing, or social analysis, goes beyond first impressions, which tend to yield incomplete pictures. An observer's first impressions are often influenced by his or her expectations and assumptions and based on limited information. Catholic social ethicists Peter

Henriot and Joe Holland define social analysis as "the effort to obtain a more complete picture of a social situation by exploring its historical and structural relationships."[5] Whereas historical analysis considers how a situation developed and changed over time, structural analysis assesses how structures such as the economy, politics, and social and cultural norms relate to the situation. Social analysts also consider who makes decisions affecting people in the situation and the values underlying the decisions. Henriot and Holland point out that social situations are complex and that the results of one's analysis is always limited.[6] Despite this, social analysis can help people see a situation more accurately than they could based on impressions, and this analytical seeing can lead to more effective judgments and actions.

Judge: Ethical Reflection

The second step, judging, involves evaluating a situation in light of guiding principles that define what is good and right, which can be drawn from any number of sources—religious doctrine, scriptures, cultural mores, philosophical perspectives, the teachings of inspirational figures. The goal of this step is to formulate a response to a problematic social situation.

Individuals evaluate the data differently, in part, because of differences in their values, priorities, and visions of what is good and right. Judging involves selecting a set of principles to use as criteria for evaluation, but it also involves recognizing that no one approaches a reality as a blank slate and assessing one's own beliefs and values and how they shape one's judgments.

Reflection makes explicit the values, commitments, and beliefs that are constantly shaping how a person relates to the world. In doing so, it challenges people to be cognizant of how they judge what they see and also whether or not what they see in the world *and* how they act in the world conforms to their deepest convictions.

---

5. Joe Holland and Peter Henriot, *Social Analysis: Linking Faith and Justice* (Maryknoll, NY: Orbis and Washington, DC: Center of Concern, 1983), 14.

6. Ibid., 15–16.

Act: Charity and Justice

Seeing and judging lead to step three—acting. The concepts of charity and justice help distinguish types of action. Charity responds to people's immediate needs, often for food, shelter, safety, and clothing. It tends to flow from a spirit of altruism and generosity or a feeling of compassion for other people. Justice aims to address the reasons why people are without adequate resources and usually requires long-term collaborative efforts with community members. This is because acting to bring about justice can involve changing systems, policies, and institutions. People who work for justice are often motivated by a sense of obligation to a vision of goodness, justice, and fairness. Charity and justice are not isolated actions and so one's response to a particular situation may involve both. However, distinguishing between charity and justice can be a helpful reminder that both aims are important and incomplete without the other. Justice without charity can downplay the importance of meeting people's immediate needs. Charity without justice can ignore structural inequalities that set up the need for charity in the first place.

Service, Learning, and the See-Judge-Act Process

Many people associate the term *service* primarily with charitable acts aimed at meeting immediate needs such as providing meals, clothing, or shelter to people living in poverty. These actions are sometimes referred to as direct service; however, the term *service* also encompasses actions aimed at bringing about justice. One type of justice-oriented service is advocacy, using one's voice to speak on behalf of someone who lacks social, political, and economic influence. For example, someone might serve hotel workers trying to form a union by writing letters to the hotel management in support of the workers' struggle. Justice-oriented service can involve empowering individuals and communities to create structural changes. Service as empowerment might involve helping residents of a marginalized neighborhood develop a community garden. Take a moment to consider your understanding of the term *service*. How does your understanding relate to direct service, advocacy, and empowerment?

How have experiences of providing or receiving service influenced your perspective?

Learning by Serving

Many college and university students today have opportunities to participate in courses that combine service with class instruction, discussions with classmates, and academic research. Learning by serving, often referred to as service learning, is an experiential educational methodology that connects students' service to specific learning objectives by engaging students in critical thinking and reflection.

Educator Andrew Furco, known for his work in the area of experiential and service learning, locates service learning within a spectrum of service and experiential learning activities according to focus (either on service or learning) and beneficiary (the recipient of the service or the provider). Service learning, Furco stresses, is unique in its balance of focus and beneficiary. Unlike volunteer work, which lacks the explicit educational intention, service learning benefits the students by enabling them to achieve the learning outcomes of the course. Unlike an internship, which focuses on the professional development of the student, service learning places as much emphasis on the interests of those served as the student.[7] Effective service learning is characterized by relationships of mutual respect between all participants—leaders of service organizations, those served by the organizations, students, and teachers.

Effective service learning[8] is related to the process of seeing, judging, and acting. First, students engaged in service learning carry out social analysis to adequately see a situation and to uncover assumptions and stereotypes that bias their observations. Second, students learn to judge situations and to draw meaning from service

---

7. Andrew Furco, "Service Learning: A Balanced Approach to Experiential Education," in *Introduction to Service-Learning Toolkit: Resources for Faculty* (Providence, RI: Campus Compact, 2001), 10.

8. John Eby identifies a number of pitfalls associated with service learning while also offering suggestions for making service learning successful. See John Eby, "Why Service-Learning Is Bad," (March, 1998) available online at *http://www.messiah.edu/external_programs/agape/servicelearning/SLResources.html*.

experiences through critical thinking and reflecting. Third, students consider how their seeing and judging leads to action.

Seeing in Service-Learning Settings

In a traditional classroom, textbooks and lectures are the primary facilitators of learning. In a service-learning course, the community outside the classroom functions something like a required text, raising questions and presenting new ways of thinking. Just as different individuals encounter texts differently, they also encounter communities differently based on their unique set of experiences, assumptions, and values. It is widely accepted in contemporary theories of learning that a person's background knowledge shapes the way he or she sees and understands reality. This suggests that before beginning service in a community, service learners should consider their knowledge about the community and on what this knowledge is based. Students might consider the following: (1) one's relationship to the people in the community; (2) any personal experiences related to the community; (3) one's existing knowledge of the community; (4) aspects of the community one has no or inadequate knowledge of; (5) what one hopes to learn from the people in the community.

Service learning provides students with an opportunity to enter into relationships that will challenge them to reflect on who they are and what they bring—knowledge, values, assumptions, biases, ideas, convictions—to the encounter with the community in which they serve. This reflection prepares students to see the situation of those they serve more clearly and to engage in effective social analysis.

Judging Situations Encountered in Service-Learning Settings

Experience in a service-learning setting alone does not guarantee learning. In fact, experience without reflection often confirms one's expectations about a situation rather than expands one's understanding. Reflection on service experiences and social situations can take many forms—written and oral, within groups or as individuals. One basic structure for facilitating reflection involves asking questions that prompt a movement from descriptive (what?) to interpretive (so what?) to contextual (now what?) understanding. Descriptive questions invite consideration of relevant facts or events in the service-learning experience. What happened? Interpretive questions move to the realm of significance for the learner. What do these facts or events mean? Finally, application questions invite learners to identify implications of their interpretations of situations encountered in service-learning settings. How does this knowledge shape future plans or contribute to a bigger picture?[9]

Reflection permits service to take the participants into a deeper realm where the service brings to light new understandings about situations and about the course content. "Reflection activities direct the student's attention to new interpretations of events and provide a means through which the community service can be studied and interpreted, much as a text is read and studied for deeper understanding,"[10] according to educators Robert Bringle and Julie Hatcher. Thinking of the context of service as a required text reinforces the importance of connecting service experiences to learning outcomes of the course. In a course on Catholic social thought, for example, service learners might reflect on their service experience and the situation of those served in light of the Gospels and the Catholic Church's teaching about justice. They might also gain new insight into the Gospel message and the Church's teaching by observing others putting the principles underlying this message and teachings into practice.

Acting in a Service-Learning Setting

When students are involved in a service-learning setting they are usually engaged in some type of service that involves action, but not all of this action is related to the third step of the process. The action that is the third step of the see-judge-act process refers to actions deliberately undertaken to correct an unjust situation following social analysis and ethical judgment or reflection. This action differs from service-oriented action that students may engage in prior to analysis and reflection, actions often undertaken in conjunction with seeing and judging. On the surface, however, these different actions

---

9. Julie Reed and Christopher Koliba, "Facilitating Reflection: A Manual for Leaders and Educators," available online at *http://www.uvm.edu/~dewey/reflection_manual/index.html*.

10. Robert Bringle and Julie Hatcher, "Reflection in Service-Learning: Making Meaning of Experience" in *Introduction to Service Learning Toolkit*, 114.

may appear the same. A student may arrive at a service-learning setting early in the semester and be asked to tutor a young student, perhaps alongside a person who has assessed and judged a situation and committed to regular service as a tutor to give younger students an opportunity for a better education.

Motivation for Serving

Because one's motivation to serve can influence his or her approach to service and affect their relationships with recipients of service, it is important to consider one's motivation before beginning service learning. Service learners should consider the following questions: What are your motivations for taking a service-learning course? What kinds of service are you drawn to and why? What do you hope to accomplish through service? What do you hope to take away from the service?

Motivations for participating in service learning vary. For some students, service is a requirement or a strongly encouraged résumé-enhancing activity. In this context it is especially important to keep the goal of mutuality at the forefront of the service-learning relationship so the community partners' interests are valued and the service is not solely perceived as a means to one's personal ends.

Examining one's motivations to serve can also be helpful in reflecting on the preconceptions about the community. Recall that this is the first step in *seeing* the community adequately. When service is understood as a way to fulfill an unmet need of the community or remedy a problem in the community, the primary focus going into the community can be on the need or the problem. This can deflect one's attention away from the community's strengths and resources. John McKnight and John Kretzmann offer a helpful tool to avoid focusing on a community's deficiencies. In their model of "Asset-Based Community Development," they suggest working with communities to identify the resources and skills that already exist in their neighborhoods and building on those strengths.[11] This approach to service is particularly helpful in service learning because

---

11. John L. McKnight and John P. Kretzmann, *Building Communities from the Inside Out: A Path toward Finding and Mobilizing a Community's Assets* (Evanston, IL: Northwestern University Institute for Policy Research, 1993).

it not only empowers the community but it also helps the learner gain a more adequate understanding of the community.

See-Judge-Act and the Catholic Social Tradition

Many educators incorporate service learning in courses designed to introduce students to the Catholic social tradition—the Catholic Church's tradition of addressing social issues through teaching and actions. When the process of see-judge-act is made explicit in such courses, the process can serve as an effective tool for promoting learning for students and improving situations for those who are served. This is because the see-judge-act process can lead to changes in unjust situations, but, also, the individuals engaged in seeing, judging, and acting have the opportunity to learn much through the process. In ongoing service learning, the see-judge-act process takes on a cyclical rather than linear character. Henriot and Holland note that the action that emerges out of observation and reflection shapes subsequent seeing, judging, and acting.[12]

In 1961, Pope John XXIII identified in *Mater et magistra* (*Christianity and Social Progress*) the process of seeing, judging, and acting as a way to bring the church's teachings on social matters to bear in concrete situations:

> The teachings in regard to social matters for the most part are put into effect in the following three stages: first, the actual situation is examined; then, the situation is evaluated carefully in relation to these teachings; then only is it decided what can and should be done in order that the traditional norms may be adapted to circumstances of time and place. These three steps are at times expressed by the three words: *observe, judge, act*. (No. 236)

John XXIII presents Catholic social teaching as a set of norms to apply to specific circumstances. This text is designed to help service learners do just that by moving from universal principles to concrete application. The text presents principles drawn from the Catholic

---

12. Holland and Henriot, *Social Analysis*, 8.

social tradition and encourages readers to apply them to issues using the methodology of see-judge-act. By presenting Catholic social thought in this way, the text invites students to discover the meaning and significance of this thought in relation to concrete situations they may be familiar with through service learning.

This text, in chapter 1, provides an overview of the Catholic social tradition and introduces the Catholic Church's official social teachings. The remaining chapters, chapters 2 through 8, each feature a major principle drawn from these teachings. The chapters, designed especially for readers engaged in service learning, provide information and tools for using the principles of Catholic social teaching as a basis for evaluating unjust situations and identifying actions aimed at promoting justice.

chapter 1

Overview of the Catholic Social Tradition

The Catholic social tradition (CST), broadly understood, refers to the thoughts, actions, and teachings that have emerged as members of the Catholic Church have responded to social injustices throughout history. This chapter will briefly discuss Catholic social thought and action and then will explore in more detail the Catholic Church's modern-era social teaching, the teaching that this text invites readers to learn about and apply to social problems encountered in service-learning situations using the see-judge-act process. The chapter will introduce the major documents that comprise CST and explore the sources that inform it, its methodology, and the major principles it articulates.

Catholic Social Thought and Action

Christians have thought about and acted on the implications of the gospel message for their relationships since the beginnings of the church. This message includes a call to Christians to love both God and neighbor: "You shall love the Lord, your God, with all your heart, with all your soul, and with all your mind. You shall love your neighbor as yourself" (Matthew 22:37, 39). Christians have wrestled to understand what the love of neighbor means and what actions it demands. Catholic social thought, in its broadest sense, refers to the ongoing reflection on the social implications of Christian discipleship—being a follower of Jesus Christ. Catholic social thought emerges through the work of many people, including church leaders, theologians, ethicists, leaders of movements for social change, and the many other Catholics trying to live out their faith in the world.

Listed here is a small sampling of key figures who have contributed to Catholic social thought and action in recent centuries. These people have worked to bring about a more equitable and just world; in this they epitomize the see-judge-act process.

Wilhelm Emmanuel von Kettler. Von Kettler (1811–1877) was the archbishop of Mainz, Germany, during the emergence of modern Catholic social teaching in Europe. In the aftermath of the Industrial Revolution, he encouraged fellow Catholics to address the social and economic problems of the day. He inspired the work of the Fribourg Union, a predominantly lay Catholic think-tank that defended the rights of workers and the right to private property while advocating for an alternative to unfettered capitalism and socialism.

John Ryan. Ryan (1869–1945), a Catholic priest and economist, applied insights of Catholic social teaching to social problems in the United States in the early twentieth century. He taught moral theology at the Catholic University of America and published writings that defended a worker's right to employment, a living wage, and just working conditions. Many of his ideas are also found in Franklin D. Roosevelt's New Deal, which put into place many safety nets still present in American society.

Jacques Maritain. Maritain (1882–1973), a French philosopher influenced by the work of Thomas Aquinas, had a lasting impact on modern Catholic theology and ethics. His writings on human dignity and freedom contributed to the Catholic Church's embrace of human rights and democracy.

Dorothy Day. Day (1897–1980) is regarded by many as one of the most important activists in the history of American Catholicism. Along with Peter Maurin, she established the Catholic Worker movement in 1933 as a way to promote social justice, peace, and simplicity. Her thoughts on nonviolence, hospitality, and solidarity with people living in poverty have made an important contribution to the Catholic social tradition.

Joseph Cardinal Bernardin. Bernardin (1928–1996), a bishop from Chicago, inspired the Catholic Common Ground Initiative, which encourages collaboration among all Catholics on important social and political issues. He challenged Catholics to transcend partisan politics and embrace a consistent ethic of life—an ethic that opposes abortion, the death penalty, war, euthanasia, and poverty by defending human dignity across the entire life span and all circumstances.

Blessed Mother Teresa of Calcutta. Mother Teresa (1910–1997), founder of the Missionaries of Charity and winner of the 1979 Nobel Peace Prize, dedicated her life to serving people living in extreme poverty in Calcutta. She consistently related her care for the most vulnerable to her love for Christ.

Gustavo Gutierrez. Gutierrez (1928–), a Catholic priest from Peru, is considered by many to be the "father of liberation theology." His theology, which emphasizes God's commitment to the liberation of oppressed people through the transformation of unjust social structures, is rooted in his observation of the reality of poverty in Latin America. Liberation theology's insistence on the preferential option for the poor has made a lasting impact on the Catholic social tradition.

Dorothy Stang. Stang (1931–2005), a Catholic sister from Ohio, spent thirty years in Brazil, advocating for economic justice and environmental sustainability in the Amazon. Her vocal opposition to logging and ranching practices that destroyed the rain forest and displaced local farmers led to her assassination in 2005. She dedicated her life to caring for creation and working for environmental justice.

Helen Prejean. Prejean (1939–) is a Catholic sister and leader in the US movement to abolish the death penalty and reform the prison system. Her advocacy is rooted in her experience ministering to inmates on death row and witnessing their executions.

The nine people highlighted—men and women; young and old; lay, ordained, or vowed members of religious communities—have dedicated themselves to the Catholic social mission in different ways, including through direct service, advocacy, education, prayer, and leadership. They each illuminate multiple expressions of charity and work for justice and highlight the importance of each in the Catholic social tradition. For example, Mother Teresa's compassionate service to the impoverished and Gustavo Gutierrez's prophetic truth telling in the face of oppression have both revealed something about what it means to love one's neighbor. The sampling of people and their contributions also reveals the practical orientation of Catholic social thought. Most of these individuals are remembered not only for their ideas about social justice but also for their actions.

The Catholic social tradition has been shaped by well-known individuals but also by untold numbers of other people whose actions have helped to bring about justice. Many of these people—lay, ordained, and vowed religious—have worked in association with parishes and dioceses and with Catholic movements and organizations. Listed here is a small sampling of organizations whose work provides examples of Catholic social action:

The Society of Saint Vincent DePaul. Founded in 1833 when French law student Frederick Ozanam gathered a group of lay Catholics together to serve the needs of people living in poverty, this society has grown into an international association of over six-hundred-thousand men and women who promote charity and social justice by providing food, shelter, clothing, and care to people in need. Since its origin, the Society of Saint Vincent DePaul has emphasized the importance of person-to-person assistance. Web site: *www.svdpusa.org/.*

Pax Christi. This international organization dedicated to peace-making originated in France through the initiative of lay Catholics who began gathering together to pray for peace. Pax Christi today offers resources for prayer and spirituality as well as education and advocacy related to peacemaking. It welcomes pacifists and just-war advocates while promoting the rights of conscientious objectors, nonviolent conflict resolution, and disarmament. Web site: *www.paxchristi.org.*

The Center of Concern. This center engages in analysis, education, and advocacy for the promotion of social justice. Located in Washington, DC, the center works to influence US policies, especially those impacting global justice. Though it is autonomous, ecumenical, and interreligious, the center began in 1971 through the collaboration of the United States Conference of Catholic Bishops (USCCB) and the Society of Jesus (Jesuits) and is rooted in the Catholic social tradition. Web site: *www.coc.org.*

Network. Network is a nationally recognized Catholic lobbying group based in Washington, DC, and informed by Catholic social teaching. Network promotes just policies related to immigration, healthcare, the environment, and the economy. It was founded in 1972 following a meeting of US Catholic sisters and continues to draw on the experiences of women religious involved in direct service and social justice work in the United States. Web site: *www. networklobby.org.*

The Ignatian Solidarity Network. This network promotes justice education and advocacy opportunities for people affiliated with Jesuit ministries. Their Ignatian Family Teach-In for Justice attracts over a thousand participants each year and provides an opportunity to learn, reflect, and advocate for justice on Capitol Hill. Web site: *www. ignatiansolidarity.net.*

Catholic Charities USA. This national association of local charities, which provides basic need assistance and advocacy for millions of Americans each year, is one of the largest nonprofit organizations in the country. Catholic Charities also works closely with local Catholic parishes and the US bishops to provide adoption services and programs to strengthen families. Web site: *www.catholiccharitiesusa.org.*

Catholic Relief Services (CRS). This organization was founded in 1943 by the USCCB and remains the official humanitarian relief organization of the Catholic Church in the United States. CRS provides international aid in the form of disaster relief, microfinance programs, peacebuilding initiatives, and assistance for communities struggling with food insecurity and HIV/AIDS. Web site: *www.crs.org.*

Catholic Climate Covenant. This initiative was launched by the US bishop-sponsored Catholic Coalition on Climate Change in 2009. The Catholic Climate Covenant encourages Catholic individuals and organizations to take the Saint Francis Pledge to pray and learn about the moral dimensions of climate change, to change their lifestyle to promote environmental responsibility, and to advocate for the care for creation. Web site: *www.catholicclimatecovenant.org.*

These organizations highlight some of the issues to which Catholics have responded—poverty, violence, global inequalities, and environmental destruction—and some of the ways they have done so. The causes of social problems, such as poverty are often embedded in the political and economic structures of society, requiring not only immediate attention but also long-term solutions and widespread commitment. Organizations dedicated to social justice can facilitate such action. Bishops' conferences, dioceses, parishes, and Catholic institutions such as universities and hospitals also can facilitate action aimed at furthering justice. The many organizations dedicated to putting Catholic social thought into action extend the reach of the Catholic Church beyond its membership and often present an opportunity to collaborate with Christians who are not Catholic, adherents of other religious and nonreligious groups, and individuals.

Catholic Social Teaching

In addition to thoughts and actions, the Catholic social tradition includes teachings. The term *Catholic social teaching* (*CST*) is commonly used to refer specifically to modern-era teachings issued officially by the Catholic Church, beginning with the social encyclical, *Rerum novarum* (*On the Condition of Labor*), promulgated by Pope Leo XIII in 1891. Many of the major writings that make up CST are papal encyclicals, which are substantial letters issued by a pope intended for wide circulation. Other major writings of CST are issued by groups of bishops, gathered in councils or synods, in conjunction with the pope. There is no official list of documents that make up Catholic social teaching, but there is broad consensus about the writings CST includes. The following list of major documents generally considered to comprise CST provides the Latin title and English title of each document along with its date, source, context, and major themes:

- *Rerum novarum* (*On the Condition of Labor*), 1891, Pope Leo XIII. Responding to industrialization and the emergence of capitalism in Europe, Leo XIII defends the right to just wages, fair working conditions, and the formation of workers' unions. Responding to socialism, the pope defends the right to private property and the importance of religion.
- *Quadragesimo anno* (*The Reconstruction of Social Order*), 1931, Pope Pius XI. Writing during the Great Depression and the rise of fascism in Europe, Pius XI argues for subsidiarity as guide for the government to protect the common good (in CST this means the flourishing of all) without overpowering local communities.
- *Mater et magistra* (*Christianity and Social Progress*), 1961, Pope John XXIII. Observing an increasingly interconnected world, John XXIII argues for solidarity between nations. He argues

specifically for the protection for traditional agricultural workers in the context of rapid economic changes.

- *Pacem in terris* (*Peace on Earth*), 1963, Pope John XXIII. In the context of the global arms race of the 1960s, John XXIII advocates for peace and disarmament. He claims that protecting human rights, which he observes to be embedded in human nature, is the foundation of peace.

- *Gaudium et spes* (*Pastoral Constitution on the Church in the Modern World*), 1965, Second Vatican Council. The council declares that the church and world are linked in human history, and the gospel remains relevant in the modern age as it gives meaning to human existence. The text defends the dignity of the human person against discrimination and modern threats to human life.

- *Populorum progressio* (*The Development of Peoples*), 1967, Pope Paul VI. Recognizing the urgent problem of global inequalities in the aftermath of colonization, Paul VI argues for integral human development that promotes the economic, social, cultural, and spiritual flourishing of all.

- *Octogesima adveniens* (*A Call to Action*), 1971, Pope Paul VI. The pope challenges the world to recognize the roots of inequalities and promote political and economic justice on national and international levels. He invites the church around the world to participate in applying CST to local contexts.

- *Justice in the World*, 1971, Synod of Bishops. Observing structural injustices and revolutionary uprisings in Latin America, the synod promotes the preferential concern for the poor. The synod declares the work for justice to be an essential part of promoting the gospel.

- *Laborem exercens* (*On Human Work*), 1981, Pope John Paul II. Recognizing that both capitalism and communism can diminish worker's dignity, the pope advocates for workers' rights and presents a personalist (person-centered) understanding of work.

- *Sollicitudo rei socialis* (*On Social Concern*), 1987, Pope John Paul II. Observing the widening gap between rich and poor nations, the pope calls for international solidarity. He denounces global economic systems that oppress impoverished nations to benefit the wealthy.

- *Centesimus annus* (*On the Hundredth Anniversary of* Rerum Novarum), 1991, Pope John Paul II. Commemorating *Rerum novarum*, the pope critiques both socialist collectivism for undermining personal freedom and unrestrained capitalism for placing competition above the needs of the impoverished.
- *Caritas in veritate* (*Charity in Truth*) 2009, Pope Benedict XVI. Commemorating *Populorum progressio* (*The Development of Peoples*), Benedict XVI addresses challenges to development in the context of globalization. Specifically, he argues that solidarity and a spirit of gratuitousness are needed to promote economic and environmental justice.

Catholic social teaching developed and will continue to develop in response to particular social issues, so over time the body of official teaching grows and new insights emerge. Central ideas, however, recur throughout the teachings, as the documents' authors aim to apply fundamental principles to particular historical situations. For example, the principle of human dignity that guided Leo XIII's response to industrialization in 1891 informed Benedict XVI's response to globalization over one hundred years later.

The remainder of the chapter will explore some of the sources that inform CST, the methodology the authors of CST employ, and major principles CST articulates.

Sources of Catholic Social Teaching

Catholic social teaching is rooted in principles drawn from the Old and New Testaments, the doctrines of the Catholic Church, and the work of theologians. Catholic social teaching, however, has never relied solely on Christian sources, drawing on philosophy and most recently, the social sciences. This section of the chapter will briefly highlight a few of the sources that inform CST—Scripture, theology, and a type of philosophical argumentation known as natural law.

Scripture

The Christian Scriptures, made up of the Hebrew Bible (Old Testament) and the New Testament are normative sources of Catholic social teaching. This is because the Catholic Church views the

The Second Vatican Council (1962–1965)

The Second Vatican Council, also called Vatican II, was an ecumenical council held from 1962 to 1965. When Pope John XXIII announced his plan to convene the Catholic bishops of the world for a council he used the term *aggiornamento*, an Italian word that means "updating," to describe his hope that the council would renew the Catholic Church and make it more responsive to contemporary realities. The council issued sixteen documents on topics related to the life of the Church and its relationship to the world. Some of the most significant developments at Vatican II include changes in the liturgy (including allowing Mass to be celebrated in the spoken language of the local churches rather than in Latin), greater emphasis on the importance of religious liberty, the need for reconciliation with other Christians, the importance of dialogue with people of other religious traditions, and openness to the wisdom of scientific discovery and secular ideas. *Gaudium et spes* (*Pastoral Constitution on the Church in the Modern World*), generally viewed as part of CST, was one of four major documents, called constitutions because they articulate central teachings or principles, issued by Vatican II.[1]

Old and New Testaments as the Word of God. In *Dei verbum* (*Dogmatic Constitution on Divine Revelation*), the Second Vatican Council explains the Catholic view that sacred Scripture is the Word of God, and in sacred Scripture, God speaks through human authors in a "human fashion"(no. 12). Aligned with the two ideas—that Scripture is the Word of God and that the Word is expressed through humans—the Catholic Church rejects fundamentalist understandings of the Bible. In other words, Catholics maintain that the Scriptures are inspired by God and, taken as a whole and

---

1. The three other major documents are *Lumen gentium* (*Dogmatic Constitution on the Church*), *Dei verbum* (*Dogmatic Constitution on Divine Revelation*) and *Sacrosanctum concilium* (*Constitution on the Sacred Liturgy*).

interpreted with the help of the Holy Spirit, reveal the truths of the Christian faith. At the same time, because the Scriptures are written by human authors in particular historical moments, the interpretation of Scripture must also consider the human factors expressed in the writings. Biblical scholars use several tools to arrive at a better understanding of these factors including archeology, cultural anthropology, and literary tools.

The authors of CST draw on the Scriptures for insight into fundamental principles including the meaning of social justice and the nature of the human person in relation to God. One example is John Paul II's use of the Bible to develop an understanding of human work in his encyclical, *Laborem exercens* (*On Human Work*):

> When man, who had been created "in the image of God . . . male and female" (Gen 1:27) hears the words: "Be fruitful and *multiply, and fill the earth and subdue* it" (Gen 1:28) even though these words do not refer directly and explicitly to work, beyond any doubt they indirectly indicate it as an activity for man to carry out in the world. Indeed, they show its very deepest essence. Man is the image of God partly through the mandate received from his Creator to subdue, to dominate, the earth. In carrying out this mandate, man, every human being, reflects the very action of the Creator of the universe. (No. 4)

Pope John Paul II interprets the biblical story of creation to articulate the relationship between human nature and work. Referring to the mandate to subdue the earth, the pope suggests that work is one of the ways that humanity participates in the creative activity of God and therefore manifests God's image in the world. In the pope's reading, the biblical text is understood in light of the whole story of creation, which highlights the unique ability of humanity to reflect God's image. The pope draws on the Bible in this case to argue for the dignity of work.

Theology

Christian theology, grounded in Scripture, the Christian tradition, and the experiences of Christians, is also a source for Catholic social teaching. The classic definition of theology offered by Saint Anselm (1033–1109) is "faith seeking understanding." This definition reveals two important dimensions of theology. First, theology presupposes the experience of faith and seeks to understand the object of faith—God. Theology is not limited to reasoning about God. Second, theology tries to make sense of reality in light of belief in God. Professional theologians take up in a more systematic way what many people of faith do throughout their lives. When individuals reflect on a significant experience such as falling in love or suffering an injury or on an aspect of nature or themselves in light of Christian belief, they sometimes come to new understandings of their faith. This reflection is theologizing. The work of theology is never ending because human beings continue to reflect on experiences in light of Christian faith.

One example of theology informing Catholic social teaching can be found in the way that Vatican II's *Gaudium et spes* (*Pastoral Constitution on the Church in the Modern World*) defines the human person:

> The root reason for human dignity lies in man's call to communion with God. From the very circumstance of his origin man is already invited to converse with God. For man would not exist were he not created by God's love and constantly preserved by it; and he cannot live fully according to truth unless he freely acknowledges that love and devotes himself to His Creator. (No. 19)

A theological understanding of the human person is different from nontheological understandings because theology tries to make sense of human existence in light of faith in God. In *Gaudium et spes*, the origin, purpose, and meaning of the human person is understood in relationship to God. These theological assumptions inform how the Catholic Church understands human dignity, resulting in different perspectives on human dignity than might be found in other approaches.

Natural Law Philosophy

Traditionally, philosophy has been an important source for Catholic thought, particularly a form of philosophical argumentation known as *natural law*. A natural law argument begins with the assumption that through the use of reason, the human mind is capable of discerning God's will in creation. Following this assumption is the claim that people's actions should conform to the order of creation as observed in the natural world and common human experience. For example, the natural inclination to preserve one's life can be used to develop a moral mandate against suicide. The advantage of a natural law argument is that it transcends religious and cultural differences. For instance, the Catholic Church uses natural law argumentation to claim the universal significance of certain teachings such as the insistence on universal human rights. The following excerpt from Pope John XXIII's encyclical on peace, *Pacem in terris* (*Peace on Earth*), provides another example of natural law informing Catholic social teaching:

> All created being reflects the infinite wisdom of God. It reflects it all the more clearly, the higher it stands in the scale of perfection. But the mischief is often caused by erroneous opinions. Many people think that the laws which govern man's relations with the State are the same as those which regulate the blind, elemental forces of the universe. But it is not so; the laws which govern men are quite different. The Father of the universe has inscribed them in man's nature, and that is where we must look for them; there and nowhere else. (Nos. 5–6)

The pope expresses the idea that God has ordered human nature, and this order should govern human relationships. From this perspective, peace will be achieved by transcending differences of opinion and following the laws of human nature.

One of the limitations of natural law is that it can fail to take into account historical and cultural differences that shape understandings of human nature. With the shift to a more historically conscious approach to theology and ethics in the second half of the twentieth century, Catholic thinkers have relied less on natural law. Many insights of natural law, however, particularly the claim that there are universal aspects of human nature, continue to inform Catholic social teaching.

Methodology of Catholic Social Teaching

In *Gaudium et spes* (*Pastoral Constitution on the Church in the Modern World*), the Second Vatican Council identified the significance of history in shaping social life and described the Catholic Church's task as reading or "scrutinizing the signs of the times and of interpreting them in the light of the Gospel" (no. 4). The signs of the times[2] are significant events, developments, struggles, and opportunities that characterize an era. The methodology of reading the signs of the times requires an ongoing process of understanding the world and discerning how to think and act in response to what is happening. Reading the signs of the times—a process with a close affinity to the see-judge-act process because both involve social analysis, ethical reflection, and informed action—is a helpful way to think about the methodology that has spurred the development of CST.

Recognizing the diverse social situations that exist in the world, in *Octogesima adveniens* (*A Call to Action*), Pope Paul VI instructs local churches to carry out a process of reading the signs of the times, or of seeing, judging, and acting, within their own contexts.

> In the face of such widely varying situations it is difficult for us to utter a unified message and to put forward a solution which has universal validity. Such is not our ambition, nor is it our mission. . . . It is up to the Christian communities to analyze with objectivity the situation which is proper to their own country, to shed on it the light of the Gospel's unalterable words and to draw principles of reflection, norms of judgment, and directives for action from the social teaching of the Church. (No. 4)

---

2. The phrase, reading the signs of the times, has biblical roots, appearing in the Gospel of Matthew (16:1–3): "The Pharisees and Sadducees came and, to test him, asked him to show them a sign from heaven. He said to them in reply, "In the evening you say, 'Tomorrow will be fair, for the sky is red'; and, in the morning, 'Today will be stormy, for the sky is red and threatening.' You know how to judge the appearance of the sky, but you cannot judge the signs of the times." The passage depicts Jesus responding to religious leaders who are skeptical about his teaching authority. In his reply, Jesus challenges them to open their eyes to what is going on around them. He points out that they can read weather patterns in the signs of nature, but they do not recognize signs of God at work in the world—healing the sick, forgiving sinners, comforting those who are suffering.

The process Paul VI describes is useful for individuals and communities seeking to understand and respond to social situations, but it also describes the type of reflection that those who have authored the Church's official teachings have engaged in.

Principles of Catholic Social Teaching

Catholic social teaching develops a number of recurring themes, which are often referred to as principles. Though no definitive listing of these principles exists, Catholic Church leaders and scholars have developed various listings helpful to those seeking to understand and apply CST.[3] The lists can provide a framework for organizing CST's central ideas, and therefore can facilitate both learning about CST and its application in particular situations.

The organization of the chapter topics in the remainder of this text reflects the list of seven major themes the USCCB articulated in 1997:[4]

The Dignity of the Human Person. The foundation for all of the Church's social teaching and ethical reflection is its theological understanding of the human person: the human person is created in the image and likeness of God. The belief that each person bears the image of God—regardless of characteristics such as race, gender, socioeconomic status, physical attributes, intelligence, behavior, or nationality—grounds Catholic social teaching's affirmation of the dignity of every individual. Furthermore, the conviction that every person bears the image of God regardless of his or her actions grounds the Church's defense of the immeasurable worth of each individual, despite their worse actions and beyond their greatest achievements.

---

3. For example, the Pontifical Council for Justice and Peace lists four major principles (human dignity, solidarity, subsidiarity, and the common good) in *The Compendium for the Social Doctrine of the Church* (Libreria Editrice Vaticana, 2004). Social ethicist, Thomas Massaro names nine key themes of Catholic social teaching (the dignity of the human person and human rights; solidarity, common good and participation; family life; subsidiarity and the proper role of government; property ownership: rights and responsibilities; the dignity of work, rights of workers, and support for labor unions; colonialism and economic development; peace and disarmament; and option for the poor and vulnerable) in his book *Living Justice: Catholic Social Teaching in Action* (Lanham, MD: Rowman and Littlefield, 2011).

4. See USCCB, *Sharing Catholic Social Teaching: Challenges and Directions* (Washington, DC: USCCB, 1997).

Call to Family, Community, and Participation. Catholic social teaching recognizes that people participate in various communities, including families, neighborhoods, and nations. Because the family provides the primary experience of community for most people, the Catholic Church emphasizes the importance of supporting families.

The Dignity of Work and the Rights of Workers. The Catholic social tradition affirms the dignity of work and the rights of workers, including the right to a living wage and the right to form labor unions. CST has consistently challenged economic systems that exploit people for their labor or place the value of profit over the value of the human person.

Option for the Poor and Vulnerable. The option for those who are poor and vulnerable calls for putting the needs of certain people first. Social injustices such as poverty that hinder human development create the conditions in which people are prevented from participating in society. The common good, defined in this context by the flourishing of all, cannot be achieved when individuals are marginalized. Empowering everyone to participate strengthens the common good.

Solidarity. Upholding the dignity of all individuals and empowering them to participate fully in community requires solidarity; a recognition that all people are interconnected and a commitment to work for the good of all people. Solidarity affirms the social nature of the human person and the interdependence of creation. As an ethical stance, solidarity goes beyond the observation that people are interconnected to the conviction that people are responsible for one another.

Care for Creation. This theme emphasizes human beings responsibility toward the whole of creation—human and nonhuman. CST advocates for environmental justice, recognizing that marginalized people (through situations such as poverty or racism) are disproportionately affected by environmental degradation.

Rights and Responsibilities. The Catholic Church teaches that human rights flow from human dignity, making them universal and intrinsic. The Church also teaches that the human person is social by nature and meant to live in relationship with others. Therefore, the Church emphasizes responsibilities alongside rights.

Applications of Catholic Social Teaching in the United States

The major writings of CST described earlier in the chapter are universal in scope, which means the pope or bishops who issued them intended to speak to the entire church and in some cases the world. The leaders of local churches are responsible for applying the universal teachings to situations that arise in local settings. The USCCB has carried out this responsibility by addressing numerous social, economic, and political issues particular to the United States. This list of selected writings illustrates the range diversity of topics the USCCB addressed in recent decades through official statements:

- *Brothers and Sisters to Us, Pastoral Letter on Racism,* 1979
- *The Challenge of Peace: God's Promise and Our Response,* 1983
- *Economic Justice for All,* 1986
- Labor Day Statements, published annually since 1986
- *Renewing the Earth: An Invitation to Reflection and Action on Environment in Light of Catholic Social Teaching,* 1991
- *The Harvest of Justice Is Sown in Peace,* 1993
- *Called to Global Solidarity,* 1997
- *A Fair and Just Workplace: Principles and Practices,* 1999
- *Forming Consciences for Faithful Citizenship,* published before each presidential election since 1999
- *Global Climate Change: A Plea for Dialogue, Prudence, and the Common Good,* 2001
- *A Place at the Table,* 2002
- *"For I Was Hungry and You Gave Me Food:" Catholic Reflections on Food, Farmers, and Farmworkers,* 2003
- *Strangers No Longer: Together on a Journey of Hope, A Pastoral Letter Concerning Migration from the Catholic Bishops of Mexico and the United States,* 2003

Looking Ahead

The seven remaining chapters of this text are designed to help service learners understand CST's central principles, gain insight into how these principles have been applied to particular situations by the USCCB, and prepare to apply the principles to situations they are familiar with, using the see-judge-act process.

Each chapter begins by briefly introducing a principle of CST and offering two sets of reflection questions designed to help readers identify their prior knowledge, assumptions, and expectations related to the principle and to an issue the chapter will explore in relation to the principle and consider how these may influence what they see in service-learning settings. Next, each chapter presents more detailed information about the principle in CST, and then considers how the USCCB applied the principle to an issue in the United States. Next, the chapters draw on social science data and insights from Christian ethics that may help readers begin the process of analyzing a contemporary social situation with which they are familiar. The chapters continue with a summary followed by a fictionalize vignette drawn from an actual service-learning setting and a series of questions designed to help readers practice aspects of the see-judge-act process. The questions encourage readers to draw on principles of Catholic social teaching as a resource for evaluating social situations and to actions that might further the goal of promoting social justice. Each chapter concludes with suggestions for further reading and research.

For Further Reading

Bergman, Roger. *Catholic Social Learning: Educating the Faith That Does Justice*. New York: Fordham University Press, 2010.

Brady, Bernard. *Essential Catholic Social Thought*. Maryknoll, NY: Orbis Press, 2008.

Deberri, Edward, and James Hug. *Catholic Social Teaching: Our Best Kept Secret*. Fourth edition. Maryknoll, NY: Orbis Press, 2003.

Dorr, Donal. *Option for the Poor, Option for the Earth: Catholic Social Teaching.* Twentieth Anniversary Edition. Maryknoll, NY: Orbis Press, 2012.

Himes, Kenneth, ed. *Modern Catholic Social Teaching: Commentaries and Interpretations.* Washington, DC: Georgetown University Press, 2005.

Massaro, Thomas. *Living Justice: Catholic Social Teaching in Action.* Lanham, MD: Rowman & Littlefield, 2011.

Mich, Marvin Krier. *Catholic Social Teaching and Movements.* Second Printing. Mystic, CT: Twenty-Third Publications, 2000.

———. *The Challenge and Spirituality of Catholic Social Teaching.* Expanded Edition. Maryknoll, NY: Orbis Press, 2011.

Defending Human Dignity against Discrimination

Introduction

Catholic social teaching (CST) affirms the innate value and dignity of every person and recognizes that people express their dignity through various social activities, including participating in family life; working; exercising one's civic responsibilities; and expressing one's creativity. CST also recognizes that human dignity can be diminished or obscured when aspects of social life exploit people or suppress their freedom to participate in economic or political life. However, Catholic teaching maintains that even if a person's dignity is overlooked or denied by social conditions, it cannot be taken away. CST aims to promote a society that respects each person by denouncing aspects of social life that disregard human dignity. The *Compendium of the Social Doctrine of the Church* summarizes well the idea that affirming human dignity lies at the center of Catholic social thought:

> *The whole of the Church's social doctrine, in fact, develops from the principle that affirms the inviolable dignity of the human person.* In her manifold expressions of this knowledge, the Church has striven above all to defend human dignity in the face of every attempt to redimension or distort its image; moreover she has often denounced the many violations of human dignity. (No. 107)[1]

---

1. Pontifical Council for Justice and Peace, *The Compendium of the Social Doctrine of the Church* (Libreria Editrice Vaticana, 2004).

Reflect on your understanding of the CST's defense of human dignity and, if possible, relate this understanding to a service-learning setting with which you may be familiar. This might include a community organization your school has a relationship with, a social context in which you serve, the life situation of people with whom you work, or another aspect of service learning.

- How do you define dignity? What is the relationship between dignity and respect? What people, experiences, and beliefs have shaped your understanding of human dignity?
- What does it mean to live with dignity? What social conditions allow people to grow in dignity? What social conditions violate human dignity?
- Identify specific ways you may have seen people expressing and honoring human dignity in a service-learning setting. Also, identify ways you may have seen people diminish or disregard the dignity of others.

Some of the most insidious violations of human worthiness or dignity are rooted in the erroneous belief that certain people are inferior to others because of their race, ethnicity, gender, or sexuality. Such attitudes have given rise to unjust social structures that diminish people's ability to develop their potential and fully participate in society. This chapter will highlight racism, one of the many "isms"—attitudes of superiority such as sexism, classism, ageism, ethnocentrism—that perpetuate social injustice. Although the history of the Catholic Church in the United States reveals examples of complacency and even participation with racist structures, the United States Conference of Catholic Bishops (USCCB) today draws on CST to issue a strong critique of racism in the United States. Consider the significance of race in your life and in service-learning sites with which you may be familiar.

- Have you thought about race a lot in your life? Where did you learn about racial differences? What role does it play in your identity and your relationship to others?
- Has a service-learning experience prompted you to think differently about race? If so, has your thinking surfaced any

assumptions or challenged any racial stereotypes of which you were unaware?

* Can you identify ways that racism has affected the community in which you live? Have you met people in a service-learning setting who have been affected by racism? If so, have you been able to discern attitudes or structures that perpetuate racism in these contexts?

This chapter introduces the principle of human dignity in CST by tracing the principle's development from the early social encyclical *Rerum novarum* (*On the Condition of Labor*, 1891) to the Second Vatican Council's *Gaudium et spes* (*Pastoral Constitution on the Church in the Modern World*, 1965) and finally to Pope John Paul II's *Evangelium vitae* (*The Gospel of Life*, 1995). Then it highlights how the USCCB has applied CST on human dignity to racism in the Unites States by analyzing the bishops' pastoral letter *Brothers and Sisters to Us* (1979) and by examining the work of two of the five USCCB subcommittees dedicated to cultural diversity in the Catholic Church. Next, the chapter draws on social science data and the work of a contemporary Catholic ethicist to help service learners begin to analyze and address racism in the United States today. The final section of the chapter provides a summary followed by a vignette drawn from an actual service-learning setting and a series of questions designed to help readers become more familiar with the see-judge-act process.

Human Dignity in Catholic Social Teaching

Early Catholic Social Teaching on Human Dignity

The early social encyclicals evoke the principle of human dignity to argue that human nature demands labor standards. Pope Leo XIII's *Rerum novarum* (*On the Condition of Labor*), for example, advocates for state-enforced labor standards such as a fair wages, decent working conditions, and Sunday rest. The pope roots the rights of the worker in God's will rather than the worker's individual interests or desires. He says in *Rerum novarum* (*RN*), for example,

No man may with impunity outrage that human dignity which God Himself treats with great reverence, nor stand in the way of that higher life which is the preparation of the eternal life of heaven. Nay, more; no man has in this matter power over himself. To consent to any treatment which is calculated to defeat the end and purpose of his being is beyond his right; he cannot give up his soul to servitude, for it is not man's own rights which are here in question, but the rights of God, the most sacred and inviolable of rights. (No. 40)

By emphasizing the "rights of God" over the rights of the person, Leo XIII presented an understanding of human dignity that differs from the liberal human-rights tradition that emerged out of the European Enlightenment's emphasis on individual freedom and subjectivity. By asserting the authority of human reason and elevating the importance of individual freedom, Enlightenment thinking challenged the authority of the Catholic Church while it laid the foundations of the modern human-rights tradition in the Western world. The early social encyclicals reacted to the perceived threats of modernity by criticizing individualistic understandings of the human person and human rights.

Leo XIII's understanding of human dignity as God given and therefore intrinsic to human nature echoes throughout CST. The understanding that this notion of human nature is supported by natural law provides a basis for making universal claims about human existence. Like in the early social encyclicals, contemporary CST grounds claims about human nature in natural law.

The Second Vatican Council on Human Dignity

Beginning with Pope John XXIII and Vatican II, CST has paid more attention to human subjectivity and freedom. Vatican II speaks of human nature, but it also speaks of the human existence as a mystery, offering a theological understanding of personhood that gives meaning to the principle of human dignity. In *Gaudium et spes* (*Pastoral Constitution on the Church in the Modern World*), Vatican II presents the meaning of human existence in light of a

Christian understanding of creation, redemption, and final destiny with God. The text draws on the book of Genesis, placing the human person in a special relationship with God the Creator by asserting that humanity bears God's own image and likeness. *Gaudium et spes* stresses the implications of humanity's likeness to God. The teaching implies that a person is able to know and love God and is therefore responsible for responding to God's invitation to relationship. Christians understand God as the Trinity, with the Father, Son, and Holy Spirit always coexisting in relationship. To bear the image of a relational God implies that people are social beings, not meant to live in isolation. Finally, people reflect the image of God in their freedom to make decisions in a way that the rest of creation cannot. With such freedom comes responsibility for one's decisions.

Gaudium et spes (*GS*) articulates the relationship between freedom, responsibility, and the invitation to relationship with God in its understanding of conscience. Understanding the text's treatment of conscience is essential for grasping the notion of human dignity that emerges from Vatican II:

> In the depths of his conscience, man detects a law which he does not impose on himself, but which holds him to obedience. Always summoning him to love good and avoid evil, the voice of conscience when necessary speaks to his heart: do this, shun that. For man has in his heart a law written by God; to obey it is the very dignity of man; according to it he will be judged. Conscience is the most secret core and sanctuary of a man. There he is alone with God, Whose voice echoes in his depths. (No. 16)

This understanding of conscience relates human dignity to an individual's ability to discern right from wrong and make decisions based on one's relationship with God. The council identifies the invitation to relationship with God as the foundation and rationale for the principle of human dignity. "The root reason for human dignity lies in man's call to communion with God" (*GS*, no. 19). Catholic teaching affirms that responding to God's call to relationship requires an exercise of freedom. "Hence man's dignity demands that he act according to a knowing and free choice that is personally motivated and prompted from within, not under blind internal impulse nor by mere external pressure" (*GS*, no. 17). Such an understanding of freedom is not contrary to the obligation to seek the good; rather, a person can find the good only in freedom (*GS*, no. 17).

Drawing on biblical texts, *Gaudium et spes* explains the reality of sin in the world as a result of humanity's misuse of freedom. For this reason, the text explains "all of human life, whether individual or collective, shows itself to be a dramatic struggle between good and evil" (no. 13). The Christian tradition teaches that, though humanity has weakened its relationship with God through sin, God actively seeks to restore the relationship, offering forgiveness and salvation to humanity. Christian belief in the mystery of the Incarnation, of God becoming human in the person of Jesus Christ, is integral to the Catholic Church's understanding of human dignity. The Catholic tradition maintains that the Incarnation affirmed the goodness of creation, not destroying human nature but perfecting it, "Since human nature as He assumed it was not annulled, by that very fact it has been raised up to a divine dignity in our respect too" (*GS*, no. 22). By highlighting the transcendent orientation of human existence, *Gaudium et spes* argues that God provides the ultimate meaning of human existence and the foundation of human dignity.

Within this theological framework, human dignity is established and perfected by God, and therefore cannot be earned or taken away. As a result of human existence, not human achievement, the quality of human dignity implies a fundamental equality in the value of all people. The theological understanding of personhood as presented at Vatican II has implications for the Church's teaching on human rights. *Gaudium et spes* declared, "With respect to the fundamental rights of the person, every type of discrimination, whether social or cultural, whether based on sex, race, color, social condition, language, or religion, is to be overcome and eradicated as contrary to God's intent" (no. 29). With this statement, Vatican II asserts that racial discrimination is a violation of a person's fundamental rights, which are established by God. This vision of the human person grounds the Church's argument against racism.

John Paul II and the Consistent Ethic of Life

Pope John Paul II built his social encyclicals on the Catholic theological understanding of personhood and the God-given dignity of all people affirmed at Vatican II. Throughout his writings, and particularly in *Evangelium vitae* (*The Gospel of Life*), John Paul II drew on Vatican II's theological understanding of the human person to argue for the need to revere life at all its stages and to highlight that respecting the dignity of all is a social concern.

The pope was convinced that a society's attitude toward the human person can lead to either a culture of life or a culture of death. In *Evangelium vitae* (*EV*), John Paul II states the following:

> It is not only a personal but a social concern which we must all foster: a concern to make unconditional respect for human life the foundation of a renewed society. We are asked to love and honour the life of every man and woman and to work with perseverance and courage so that our time, marked by all too many signs of death, may at last witness the establishment of a new culture of life, the fruit of the culture of truth and of love. (No. 77)

A *culture of life* is supported by a collective attitude that respects human life at all stages and opposes multiple threats to life including abortion, euthanasia, the death penalty, war, violence, and poverty. John Paul II's insight that a society's attitude toward human life at every stage leads to either a life-affirming or death-dealing culture gives rise to a concern for establishing a *consistent ethic of life*. A consistent ethic of life defends human dignity against multiple injustices, recognizing that all threats to human life stem from a distorted understanding of the human person that should be replaced with an uncompromising reverence for life.

A culture of life, as Pope John Paul presents it, not only opposes specific threats to life but it also resists attitudes that obscure the inherent value of each person. He cites individualism and materialism as characteristics of a culture of death. A materialistic and individualistic view of reality, John Paul argues, results in a distorted understanding of the human person that locates a person's value in

Joseph Cardinal Bernardin and the Consistent Ethic of Life

The phrase, *consistent ethic of life*, is most often associated with the work of Joseph Cardinal Bernardin (1928–1996). His teaching emerged alongside movements in the Catholic Church in the United States that advocated for consistency in the Church's public voice on issues such as abortion, the death penalty, nuclear war, and other threats to human life. This movement challenged Catholics and others to put political differences aside and defend human dignity. The movement also invited Catholics to consider how the Catholic Church's defense of human dignity should go beyond pro-life activities to include efforts aimed at ending social injustices that diminish the *quality* of human life, such as poverty, violence, and discrimination.

his or her "usefulness" to society. It is particularly harmful to the most vulnerable members of society:

> In the materialistic perspective described so far, interpersonal relations are seriously impoverished. The first to be harmed are women, children, the sick or suffering, and the elderly. The criterion of personal dignity—which demands respect, generosity and service—is replaced by the criterion of efficiency, functionality and usefulness: others are considered not for what they "are", but for what they "have, do and produce." This is the supremacy of the strong over the weak. (*EV*, no. 23)

A culture of life rejects this model of relationship by valuing *being* over *having* (*EV*, no. 98). By valuing people for who they are rather than what they achieve, John Paul's vision of social justice affirms the innate nature of human dignity. Affirming the innate dignity and worth of the human person allows CST to reject all forms of racism.

The United States Conference of Catholic Bishops on Racism

The Catholic Church has participated both in maintaining and dismantling the structures of racism in the United States. History reveals that the Church has perpetuated racial injustices. For example, Catholic clergy and religious orders in the United States owned African American slaves well into the nineteenth century and participated in institutionalized segregation by excluding black people from Catholic colleges and seminaries.[2] European Catholic missionaries participated in the cultural suppression and violent displacement of Native Americans during the colonization of North America.[3] At the same time, history shows that Catholics have led efforts to eradicate racism in the

John LaFarge and Thea Bowman Challenge Racism

A number of Catholic individuals stand out in the history of activism for racial justice in the United States. For example, John LaFarge, S.J., a white Jesuit priest, promoted awareness of racial injustices in the 1930s. LaFarge was a leader in developing the Catholic Interracial Council, which focused on eliminating racism through education and collaboration among black and white Catholics. Thea Bowman (1937–1990), a black Franciscan Sister of Perpetual Adoration, promoted diversity and racial justice in the Catholic Church and society by drawing on the resources of the black community. Bowman is remembered for the ways she promoted the integration of African American songs, art, and traditions into Catholic liturgy.

---

2. For a historical analysis of the Catholic Church and African American experiences, see Cyprian Davis, *A History of Black Catholics in the United States* (New York: Crossroad, 1990).

3. For a historical account of the treatment of Native Americans by Christian missionaries, see George Tinker, *Missionary Conquest: The Gospel and Native American Cultural Genocide* (Minneapolis: Fortress Press, 1993).

United States. Catholic dioceses, parishes, and religious orders provide numerous services and advocacy efforts for racial minorities today, particularly those living in poverty.

This ambivalent legacy of the Catholic Church in the United States is the starting point for the USCCB's contemporary teaching on racism. This section will explore how the USCCB has addressed racism in the United States by focusing on their 1979 pastoral letter, *Brothers and Sisters to Us*. It will also highlight the subsequent work on racism led by the USCCB committee on Cultural Diversity in the Church.

The United States Conference of Catholic Bishops' Pastoral Letter on Racism

In 1979, the USCCB issued a pastoral letter, *Brothers and Sisters to Us (BSU)*. In the letter the bishops asserted that racism is a sin and a violation of human rights:

> Racism is a sin: a sin that divides the human family, blots out the image of God among specific members of that family, and violates the fundamental human dignity of those called to be children of the same Father. Racism is the sin that says some human beings are inherently superior and others essentially inferior because of races. It is the sin that makes racial characteristics the determining factor for the exercise of human rights. (No. 9)[4]

By naming racism as a social sin and a violation of human dignity, the bishops connected the elimination of racism with the Church's mission to participate in Christ's redemptive work in the world.

In the text, the bishops identify overt and covert features of racism in the United States. Specifically, they note that racial minorities are more likely to be trapped in cycles of poverty:

> Major segments of the population are being pushed to the margins of society in our nation. As economic pressures

---

4. The paragraph numbers cited for quotes from *Brothers and Sisters to Us* reflect the author's paragraph numbering as the version of the document available on the USCCB Web site lacks both page and paragraph numbers.

tighten, those people who are often black, Hispanic, Native American and Asian—and always poor—slip further into the unending cycle of poverty, deprivation, ignorance, disease, and crime. Racial identity is for them an iron curtain barring the way to a decent life and livelihood. (No. 6)

The fact that racial minorities in the United States are more likely than white people to live in poverty reveals a connection between racial injustice and economic injustice. The bishops point out that, although enforced segregation has been overcome, making racism less overt, one does not have to look far to see signs of covert or disguised racial segregation in housing, education, and the job market. Racial minorities are excluded from certain neighborhoods and are still underrepresented at many of the best schools and top-paying jobs. These examples suggest that racial discrimination has perpetuated stereotypes and has marginalized groups of people because of their race. The bishops argue that expressions of overt and covert racial discrimination contradict one of the central teachings of Christianity—that people are equally loved by God and therefore should be treated with equal dignity and respect through both individual actions and institutional and structural policies and procedures.

The bishops develop an ethical response to racism by drawing on Scripture and the Catholic Church's tradition. They point to the Exodus story, which tells of God liberating Israel from slavery, to emphasize God's desire for freedom for oppressed people. They highlight gospel passages that reveal Jesus' commitment to justice for the poor and vulnerable to stress the need for Christians to promote justice for racial minorities. The text also points out that the nature of the church, understood to be the Body of Christ, is to serve as a sign of unity among humankind. "This is the mystery of our Church, that all men and women are brothers and sisters, all one in Christ, all bear the image of the Eternal God" (*BSU*, no. 27). As a global communion, the Catholic Church is a racially and culturally diverse community.

The USCCB points out that in the United States "all too often the Church in our country has been for many a 'white Church,' a racist institution" (*BSU*, no. 30). The USCCB acknowledges that Catholics too often have failed to participate in the mission of promoting justice through combating racism. They also acknowledge ways in which white Catholics have contributed to the problem of racial injustice: "Each of us as Catholics must acknowledge a share in the mistakes and sins of the past. Many of us have been prisoners of fear and prejudice. We have preached the Gospel while closing our eyes to the racism it condemns. We have allowed conformity to social pressures to replace compliance with social justice" (*BSU*, no. 31). Such complacency toward racism, they stress, contradicts the mission of the Catholic Church and the Christian understanding of the human person.

After naming the reality of racism and providing a theological and ethical challenge, the bishops offer practical directives for the Catholic Church in the United States to eradicate racism and promote racial justice. These include creating programs to support racial minorities to enter into leadership positions in society and in the Church, celebrating diversity through Catholic worship and liturgy, and ensuring that Catholic institutions manifest just policies and practices for people of all races. They also encourage Catholic leaders to speak out about the problem of racism, and they encourage all Catholics to participate in ecumenical, interreligious, and secular movements that promote racial justice (*BSU*, no. 45).

By identifying specific expressions of racism in the United States and challenging the Catholic Church to eliminate racism in the church and society, *Brothers and Sisters to Us* stands out as an important contribution to Catholic social thought on racial injustice. The pastoral letter has a number of limitations; however, leaving much work to be done in the promotion of justice for people of color. Specifically, respondents to the text have noted that primarily white church leaders authored the text and directed it to white church members. This is implicit in the title, with *us* referring to white Catholics who embrace people of color as *brothers and sisters*.[5] Since the publications of the letter, the bishops have worked to empower racial minorities to exercise leadership within the church. The USCCB's five subcommittees on cultural diversity carry out much of this work.

---

5. Bryan Massingale makes this point in *Racial Justice and the Catholic Church* (Maryknoll, NY: Orbis, 2010), 17.

The Committee on Cultural Diversity in the Church

In their pastoral letter on racism, the USCCB made an explicit commitment to promote racial justice in the United States and challenged all Catholics to join them in their effort. They also offered direct guidelines to promote racial justice in policies, liturgical practices, and the monetary commitments of the Catholic Church. In the years following the publication of *Brothers and Sisters to Us*, the bishops implemented a number of pastoral initiatives aimed at celebrating diversity within the Catholic Church and eliminating racism in the Church and society. Many of these efforts were supported by the USCCB's committee on Cultural Diversity in the Church. The purpose of the committee is to provide training and resources for advocacy and pastoral care that is attentive to the cultural diversity of the Church. It works with permanent subcommittees that collaborate directly with specific communities to promote their interests. There are subcommittees for African American Affairs; Asian and Pacific Affairs; Hispanic Affairs; Native American Affairs; and the Pastoral Care of Migrants, Refugees, and Travelers. Due to limited space, this chapter focuses on only two of the five subcommittees. Specifically, this section examines a small portion of the work of the subcommittee on African American Affairs and the subcommittee on Native American Affairs to provide examples of the USCCB's ongoing work and to highlight some of the challenges the Catholic Church faces today in the effort to promote awareness and respect for diversity in the Church.

Subcommittee on African American Affairs

On the twenty-fifth anniversary of *Brothers and Sisters to Us*, the USCCB's subcommittee on African American Affairs presented a report on the document's effectiveness. The report noted that though some progress has been made in realizing the Catholic Church's commitment to eliminating racism, "much work remains to be done."[6] The report noted that "the majority of American Catholics have not heard the topic of racism addressed in homilies at Mass

---

6. USCCB, "A Research Report Commemorating the Twenty-Fifth Anniversary of *Brothers and Sisters to Us:* Executive Summary," 12. Available online at *http://nccbuscc.org/saac/25threalities.shtml.*

in the past three years."[7] The report also noted that the enrollment of African American students at Catholic schools declined by fifty-thousand students in the twenty year period between 1984 and 2004 and that racial segregation at Catholic schools is often higher than that of public schools.[8] The bishops challenge Catholic leaders to "renew their commitment to speak out against racism so as to raise people's awareness of the systemic nature of this form of evil."[9]

One of the findings that troubled the committee was a lack of attention to the formation of religious leaders to serve culturally diverse churches. Studies of seminary programs in the United States showed that "many diocesan seminaries and ministry formation programs are inadequate in terms of their incorporation of the history, culture, and traditions of Black Americans."[10] This can lead to a weak relationship between religious leaders and the people they serve. The committee also suggests that it hinders the promotion of vocations among racial minorities in the Catholic Church because "black men and women, both young and old, seek in their formation programs evidence of the same culture, traditions, and liturgical styles found in their home parishes."[11] In response to its findings, the committee advocated "inculturated ministry formation" so that leaders in the Church can effectively promote the incorporation of spiritual and cultural gifts of minorities into the liturgy.[12]

The term *inculturation* in this context refers to the process by which the ministries of the Catholic Church are carried out in conversation with the cultural realities of a particular community. Attention to the dignity of diverse cultures has grown in the Church since the Second Vatican Council in *Ad gentes* (*Decree on the Missionary Activity of the Church*, 1965) stated that "The Church, in order to be able to offer all of them [non-Christians] the mystery of salvation and the life brought by God, must implant herself into these groups for the same motive which led Christ to bind Himself, in virtue of

---

7. Ibid., 2.
8. Ibid., 9–10.
9. Ibid., 12.
10. Ibid., 5.
11. Ibid.
12. Ibid., 7.

His Incarnation, to certain social and cultural conditions of those human beings among whom He dwelt" (no. 10). Understanding the Catholic Church's mission through an incarnational framework has shifted the Church's approach to missionary activity by giving attention to the goodness in local traditions, spiritualities, and cultural practices. In this framework, announcing the gospel does not devalue local cultures. This awareness has been important in developing appreciation for cultural diversity and challenging the tendency to view the manifestation of the Catholic Church in Europe as normative across cultures.

Subcommittee on Native American Affairs

Reconciling with colonial history has been a significant theme in the work of the USCCB's subcommittee on Native American Affairs. In preparation for the fifth centenary of European presence in North America, the USCCB issued a statement, "1992: A Time for Remembering, Reconciling, and Recommitting Ourselves as a People." In the text, the bishops restated their regret for the ways the Catholic Church failed to respect and protect the culture, traditions, and dignity of Native American people during European expansion in North America. The statement acknowledged that injustice toward Native Americans is not just a problem of the past and insisted that "all of us need to examine our own perceptions of Native Americans—how much they are shaped by stereotypes, distorted media portrayals, or ignorance. We fear that prejudice and insensitivity toward native peoples is deeply rooted in our culture and in our local churches."[13]

Recognizing the ways that the Catholic Church has failed to honor the gifts of Native American cultures, the text identifies inculturation as a primary challenge:

> The Church is called to bring the saving word of the Gospel to every people and culture. Our goal must be an authentic inculturation of Catholic faith within the Native American

---

13. USCCB, "1992: A Time for Remembering, Reconciling, and Recommitting Ourselves as a People" (November 1991), 3. Available online at *http://www.usccb. org/issues-and-action/cultural-diversity/native-american/resources/upload/a-time-for-remembering.pdf*.

community through a vital liturgical life, continuing educational efforts, and creative pastoral ministry which demonstrate deep respect for native culture and spiritualities and which enhance fidelity to the Catholic faith.[14]

The text states that the challenge of inculturation must be met by increased participation of Native Americans in all areas of the Church's ministry. The text notes that increasing participation of historically marginalized groups requires empowerment of those communities, which can occur in many ways but must begin with listening to the interests, aspirations, and needs of the immediate community.

The Kateri Tekakwitha Conference

Founded in 1939, the Kateri Tekakwitha Conference promotes cultural awareness and advocacy for Native American Catholics. Named after the first Native North American saint, the conference promotes leadership among Native Americans in the Catholic Church. The conference also promotes inculturation through liturgies that incorporate Native American language, music, and ritual and through meaningful catechesis that is sensitive to Native American identities and traditions.

Reading the Signs of the Times:
Racial Discrimination and White Privilege

This section will further examine racism in the United States today by drawing on the social science data and the analysis of Catholic ethicist Bryan Massingale, whose work applies Catholic social thought to this issue. This section will present the concepts of white privilege and social sin as tools for observing, understanding,

---

14. Ibid., 4.

and critiquing racism as a structural and cultural injustice in the United States.

The reality of racism cannot be isolated from other social issues. Racial discrimination and inequality are factors in many social realities that Catholic social thought examines including, for example, health care, education, immigration, economics, and work. The Pew Research Center reported in 2009 that "the median wealth of white households is 20 times that of black households and 18 times that of Hispanic households."[15] The Economic Policy Institute (EPI) adds that racial minorities are disproportionately affected by the most recent economic recession.[16] In a 2011 report, the EPI compared the current unemployment rates of multiple states and concluded that even though whites face a high unemployment rate of 10 percent, African Americans in the same states face unemployment rates of 15 to 20 percent and Hispanics face a 15 percent rate of unemployment.[17] Despite the data that points to continuing racial inequality in the United States, a 2011 Gallup poll revealed that only 19 percent of white Americans think that the government should "play a major role in improving the social and economic position of blacks."[18]

Black theologian and Catholic priest Bryan Massingale explains the ambivalence that many white people have toward racial justice through the concept of *white privilege*. Examining white privilege requires a shift in attention away from the ways that racism *disadvantages* people of color and instead focuses on how racial injustice sets up *advantages* for white people.[19] In her classic essay, "White Privilege: Unpacking the Invisible Knapsack," Peggy McIntosh proposes a number of examples of white privilege. As a white person, she observes, "I

---

15. Paul Taylor, Richard Fry, and Rakesh Kochhar, Pew Research Center Executive Summary, "Wealth Gaps Rise to Record Highs between Whites, Blacks, Hispanics" (July 26, 2011) available online at *http://www.pewsocialtrends.org/2011/07/26/wealth-gaps-rise-to-record-highs-between-whites-blacks-hispanics/*.

16. Algernon Austin, Economic Policy Institute Issue Brief no. 299 (April 20, 2011) available online at *http://www.epi.org/publication/ib299/*.

17. Ibid.

18. Frank Newport, Gallup Poll, "Whites, Blacks Differ on Government's Role in Civil Rights", (August 19, 2011), available online at *http://www.gallup.com/poll/149087/Blacks-Whites-Differ-Government-Role-Civil-Rights.aspx*.

19. Bryan Massingale, *Racial Justice and the Catholic Church* (Maryknoll, NY: Orbis, 2010), 37.

can, if I wish, arrange to be in the company of people of my race most of the time. . . . I am never asked to speak for all the people of my racial group. . . . I can take a job with an affirmative action employer without having coworkers on the job suspect that I got it because of race."[20]

Coming to terms with white privilege is crucial for overcoming the power imbalances that are engendered by racism, but it is not an easy process. Massingale observes,

> Being racially advantaged might be unwanted or undesired by individual white Americans. In fact, some white Americans are distressed when they become aware of the reality of white privilege. Regardless of an individual's desires, an 'invisible package of unearned assets' is enjoyed by white people because of the racial consciousness that is subtly pervasive in our social customs and institutions.[21]

Massingale challenges the Catholic Church to do more to address racism on a pastoral level and in official teachings. In his reading of the bishops statements on racism since *Brothers and Sisters to Us*, Massingale suggests that "the dominant approach found in recent Catholic episcopal reflection on racism is marked by (1) stress on its interpersonal manifestations; (2) a strategy of moral suasion and appeals to an enlightened conscience; and (3) calls for decency, civility, respect, and fair treatment, which will translate into improved social relationships among America's racial groups."[22] What is lacking, Massingale argues, is an examination of racism on a cultural level. Culture carries the beliefs, symbols, and stories by which a community gives meaning to its experience and passes on that shared meaning to future generations. Addressing racism on a cultural level requires challenging deeply held beliefs and reshaping the systems that perpetuate these beliefs. With the exception of a few bishops, Massingale notes that the official Catholic response to racism emphasizes the need to change attitudes and personal behavior and is missing an analysis of the systems that structure racial inequalities.

---

20. Peggy McIntosh, "White Privilege: Unpacking the Invisible Knapsack," *Peace and Freedom* (July 1989): 10–12.

21. Massingale, *Racial Justice*, 37.

22. Bryan Massingale, "James Cone and Recent Catholic Episcopal Teaching on Racism" *Theological Studies* Vol. 61:4 (December 2000): 714.

Massingale stresses the "systemic nature" of racism and notes that racism is not limited to the sins of individuals; it exists within the very fabric of society, embodied in systems that disadvantage and oppress people of color. Theologians, including Massingale, join the USCCB in identifying racism as a *social sin*. Social sin is not the same as personal sin, which emerges out of the freedom and responsibility of an individual; therefore, social sin requires a different framework to understand and address. Social sin, however, is rooted in human decisions and so cannot be separated from personal sin. Because social sin is larger than personal sin, it requires social as well as individual change. Describing social sin, Massingale states, "Social institutions and processes are not morally neutral; they reflect the values and the biases of those who create and maintain them."[23] It can be challenging to identify social sin because, as Massingale continues, "we are then born into a world already formed by these structures, and we grow up thinking that these structures and the values that they incarnate are perfectly normal and legitimate. One of the characteristics of social sin, then, is that we're often blind to its existence."[24] Massingale's work suggests that efforts to eradicate racism should consider the need for societal transformation and ecclesial transformation in addition to personal transformation.

Summary and Integration for Service Learners

The social analysis highlighted in this chapter shows that racism continues to affect social structures and cultural attitudes in the United States. Today, the USCCB draws on CST to promote racial justice in the Catholic Church and in society as a whole through teaching, service, and advocacy. CST's principle of human dignity grounds the Church's opposition to racism. This principle, as developed in the Catholic social tradition, invites an uncompromising recognition of the value of each person as a reflection of God's own image.

Now that you have read about the Catholic Church's understanding of human dignity, revisit your answers to the questions at

---

23. Bryan Massingale, "Are You a Social Sinner" interview with *U.S. Catholic, U.S. Catholic* Vol. 70:2 February 2005): 21.

24. Ibid.

the start of the chapter. Would you answer any questions differently? Does the chapter's discussion of racism in the United States shed light on social issues you may have encountered in a service-learning setting? How can the principle of human dignity help address racial injustices? Use the following vignette and questions to practice the see-judge-act process in relation to this topic.

Uncovering Racial Stereotypes

Service-Learning Vignette

A white student beginning her service learning at an afterschool program that serves low-income youth was instructed to find the school principal to get instructions for her first day of service. She went into the principal's office and encountered two women, one white and one African American, both dressed in business attire. The student introduced herself to the white woman, assuming she was the principal. The student was embarrassed to learn that the woman she approached was a teacher and the other woman was the principal. After reflecting on the interaction, the student concluded that the school must have hired an African American principal because she would be a better fit for serving low-income youth.

See: Social Analysis

- What assumptions about race may have shaped the student's interaction with the women in this vignette? Does the interaction challenge or confirm these assumptions? Do you observe evidence of white privilege in the student's assumptions?

- How might structural injustices—those embodied in the educational system, economy, media, and so on—have contributed to the student's assumptions in the vignette?

Judge: Ethical Reflection

- What attitudes, beliefs, and behaviors may have influenced the student's interaction with the principal? How does CST's principle of human dignity challenge or affirm the views and behavior of the student?

- How might the concept of *social sin* aid one's understanding of and judgments about racism? What are some of the characteristics of social sin that could be relevant in judging the vignette's scenario?

Act: Promoting Justice

- Identify actions aligned with CST's emphasis on the God-given dignity of all people that respond to the situation of people of color suffering from poverty spurred by racism.
- Following Massingale's cultural analysis of racism, what specific actions can be taken by individuals and by communities to promote a culture that celebrates racial equality and cultural diversity?

Suggestions for Further Social Analysis in a Service-Learning Context

- Research racial demographics in a selected city according to neighborhood. Do the data suggest the presence of racial segregation?
- Use census information to identify connections between race and other demographic information—income, education level, and employment—in a particular locale. Do the data suggest any connections between race, income, education level, and employment?
- Identify public and private organizations that address racial inequalities in a selected city. What social issues do they target in their promotion of racial equality? What have they identified as some of the obstacles to racial equality?

For Further Reading on Catholic Social Thought and Racism

Flynn, Harry. "In God's Image: Pastoral Letter on Racism" (2003) available online at *http://www.archspm.org/reference/pastoral-letters-detail.php?int Resource ID=158.*

George, Francis Cardinal, O.M.I. "Dwell in My Love: A Pastoral Letter on Racism"(2001) available online at *http://www.archdiocese-chgo.org/cardinal/ dwellinmylove/dwellinmylove.shtm.*

Massingale, Bryan. *Racial Justice and the Catholic Church.* Maryknoll, NY: Orbis, 2010.

Nothwehr, Dawn M. *That They May Be One: Catholic Social Teaching on Racism, Tribalism, and Xenophobia.* Maryknoll, NY: Orbis, 2008.

Phan, Peter C., and Diana Hayes, eds. *Many Faces, One Church: Cultural Diversity and the American Catholic Experience.* Lanham, MD: Rowman & Littlefield, 2005.

Justice for Immigrants:
The Call to Family, Community,
and Participation

Introduction

The Catholic social tradition recognizes that people are social by nature and that the organization of society affects how well it protects the dignity of individuals and the ability of people to form community and participate fully in society. Social life provides the context in which people either thrive or encounter obstacles that prevent them from attaining their potential, making it an important topic for Catholic social teaching (CST). The second of the United States Council of Catholic Bishops' (USCCB) seven themes of CST, the call to family, community, and participation, reflects the Church's teaching on this topic. This principle has been developed in a number of ways in the Catholic social tradition, emerging in the church's teaching on the common good, the importance of the family as a basic unit of society, and the need to overcome marginalization by allowing everyone to participate in social life. The USCCB summarizes the principle in this way:

> The person is not only sacred but also social. How we organize our society—in economics and politics, in law and policy—directly affects human dignity and the capacity of individuals to grow in community. Marriage and the family are the central social institutions that must be supported and strengthened, not undermined. We believe people have a right and a duty to participate in society, seeking together

the common good and well-being of all, especially the poor and vulnerable.[1]

Reflect on the experiences, beliefs, and values that have shaped your understanding of community.

- Name the communities with which you identify, such as family, neighborhood, church, school, interest group, team, and nation. How would you order these communities according to their significance in your life? What values and beliefs inform the order?
- What is the nature of your participation in the communities you listed in response to the previous set of questions? Identify any obstacles that may have prevented you from fully participating in any of these communities?
- Identify specific ways you may have seen the building of community in a service-learning setting. Also, identify ways you may have seen community being diminished and people's participation in community thwarted in a service-learning setting.

This chapter will explore the call to family, community, and participation by examining the Catholic Church's response to issues associated with migration, a reality that can both disrupt social life and lead to new expressions of community. This chapter will focus on the USCCB's response to migration with particular attention to the collaborative work of the US and Mexican bishops. As this chapter will highlight, the US-Mexico border provides an important context for contemporary social analysis and ethical reflection on migration in the Americas. Consider your beliefs and assumptions about migration using the following questions.

- Does your family's history inform your views on migration? Explain.
- What is the significance of citizenship and nationality for you? How do these beliefs inform your position on immigration policy? What values inform your position?

---

1. USCCB, "*Seven Themes of Catholic Social Thought*" available online at *http://www.usccb.org/beliefs-and-teachings/what-we-believe/catholic-social-teaching/seven-themes-of-catholic-social-teaching.cfm*.

- Have any service-learning settings you may be familiar with led you to examine the situation of immigrants in the United States? If so, did your examination prompt you to think differently about immigrants and the policies that affect immigration patterns and the experiences of migrants? Explain.

This chapter will examine how the call to family, community, and participation has developed as a principle of CST by highlighting writings on the common good and family life. Since the early social encyclicals, CST has insisted that people are obligated to promote the common good. Specifically, this chapter will explore how the principle informs Popes Leo XIII and Pius XI's positions on private property and supports Pope John XXIII's argument for global solidarity. With a basic understanding of the common good, the chapter will turn to the role of the family in strengthening community life. Pope John Paul II, in particular, highlighted the social dimension of the family and, using the principle of subsidiarity, suggested that strengthening families contributes to the common good from the bottom up. In the next section, the chapter will draw on the joint pastoral letter of the US and Mexican bishops to explore their application of CST to the topic of migration in the context of the Americas. Next, the chapter will draw on sociological data and the scholarship of Catholic theologian Daniel Groody to analyze the situation of undocumented workers—immigrants residing and working in the United States without legal permission from the US government. The final section of the chapter provides a summary followed by a vignette drawn from an actual service-learning setting and a series of questions designed to help readers practice aspects of the see-judge-act process.

The Call to Family, Community, and Participation in Catholic Social Teaching

Early Social Encyclicals Oppose Individualism and Collectivism

Throughout its history, CST has defended the dignity of the individual and called for meeting the needs of the community. These commitments are reflected in the Catholic social tradition's rejection of individualism—a system in which individual rights supersede community needs—and collectivism—a system of collective control over political and economic matters—in favor of an approach to social life that balances the rights and freedoms of the individual and the needs and interests of the community. This stance provides the foundation for the Catholic Church's teaching on the common good.

The early social encyclicals developed an understanding of the common good in response to the two dominant systems of the Industrial era—liberal capitalism and socialism. Pope Leo XIII critiqued liberal capitalism for promoting excessive individualism at the expense of the needs of the community. The pope also rejected the socialist alternative in fear that too much state control would promote excessive collectivism and threaten the right to private property. The concept of the common good emerges within this concern for the natural right to private property. Following his predecessor, Pope Pius XI used the principle of the common good to argue for the just limitations on private property for the sake of the community. He explained in *Quadragesimo anno* (*The Reconstruction of Social Order*, 1931) that CST defends the following:

> The twofold character of ownership, called usually individual or social according as it regards either separate persons or the common good. For they have always unanimously maintained that nature, rather the Creator Himself, has given man the right of private ownership not only that individuals may be able to provide for themselves and their families but also that the goods which the Creator destined for the entire family of mankind may through this institution truly serve this purpose. (No. 45)

Pius XI's understanding of the common good is grounded in the conviction that there is a universal purpose for created things, namely, to sustain the whole human family. This view leaves room for personal and social ownership of property. The common good refers to those goods that contribute to the thriving of the whole community. Pius XI, like Leo XIII, argues that everyone has a responsibility to foster the common good and that the state is obligated to protect the common good.

Pope John XXIII and Vatican II: The Global Common Good

Pope John XXIII builds on the foundation of the early social encyclicals by defending both the dignity of the individual and the importance of community. Writing in the 1960s, John XXIII demonstrated a heightened awareness of the global dimensions of the human community—an awareness with implications for understanding the common good. In his social encyclical *Mater et magistra* (*Christianity and Social Progress*, 1961), he pointed out that nations are increasingly interconnected. He referred specifically to the international economy, arguing that it should be regulated according to the demands of the global common good. He also suggested specific demands for individual nations and the international community. The demands of the common good on the national level include demands that nations foster as much employment as possible, eliminate inequalities, and evaluate progress in light of future generations. In *Mater et magistra* (*MM*), John XXIII states that the common good demands that the international community avoid excessive competition and promote economic growth for developing countries (nos. 79–80).

Reflecting the thought of John XXIII, the Second Vatican Council assumes an interdependent world that transcends nations. *Gaudium et spes* (*Pastoral Constitution on the Church in the Modern World*, 1965) discusses the implications of this reality for the common good:

> Every day human interdependence grows more tightly drawn and spreads by degrees over the whole world. As a result the common good, that is, the sum of those conditions of social life which allow social groups and their individual members relatively thorough and ready access to their own fulfillment, today takes on an increasingly universal complexion and consequently involves rights and duties with respect to the whole human race. Every social group

must take account of the needs and legitimate aspirations of other groups, and even of the general welfare of the entire human family. (No. 26)

Following Vatican II, CST attended to the universal complexion of the common good. This focus affects the Church's position on issues such as international development, human rights, the environment, and migration. Regarding migration, CST maintains that the common good transcends borders but that this does not mean that nations do not have the right and responsibility to regulate their borders and provide security for their citizens. According to *Gaudium et spes* (*GS*), this right, however, cannot override the responsibility to protect the "needs and legitimate aspirations of other groups" (no. 26).

Pope John Paul II on Subsidiarity and the Family

CST calls for the various levels and units of social life—family, neighborhood, town, county, state, nation—to relate according to the principle of subsidiarity. This principle calls for larger social units to solve problems and make decisions for smaller social units only if the smaller unit is unable to do so. If a smaller unit cannot or does not achieve the necessary goods to thrive, the larger community has a responsibility to take action.

In *Familiaris consortio* (*On the Role of the Christian Family in the Modern World*, 1981) Pope John Paul II draws on the principle of subsidiarity to argue for the protection of the privacy and legitimate autonomy of the family in society. According to *Familiaris consortio* (*FC*), "By virtue of this principle, the State cannot and must not take away from families the functions that they can just as well perform on their own or in free associations; instead it must positively favor and encourage as far as possible responsible initiative by families" (no. 45). John Paul II grounds this argument in the conviction that the family is the basic cell of society, because it provides the most immediate experience of relationship. Ideally, the family prepares people to participate in society by instilling the virtues necessary for social life. Family life can teach people about their responsibility toward others, and promote the virtues of solidarity, compassion, and fidelity. Because of this, society should be concerned with promoting healthy families by providing the respect and support they need to thrive. John Paul II suggests the following:

> The family has vital and organic links with society, since it is its foundation and nourishes it continually through its role of service to life: it is from the family that citizens come to birth and it is within the family that they find the first school of the social virtues that are the animating principle of the existence and development of society itself. Thus, far from being closed in on itself, the family is by nature and vocation open to other families and to society, and undertakes its social role. (*FC*, no. 42)

Based on the conviction that the family should be protected as the foundation of a healthy society, John Paul II argues for the legal recognition of specific rights of the family. Among them, he argues that families have "the right to exist and progress as a family," and he argues that families have "the right to emigrate as a family in search of a better life" (*FC*, no. 46). This understanding of the rights of the family informs the Catholic Church's position on migration, which challenges immigration policies that perpetuate family separation. For this reason, the reunification of families is one of the top priorities in the Church's stance on immigration policies.

The Catholic Church's Response to Immigration to the United States

Church of Immigrants

Immigration has been a concern for the Catholic Church in the United States since it began as a church of immigrants in the eighteenth century and as it grew as waves of Europeans, including Irish, Italians, and Germans, immigrated to the United States in the nineteenth and early twentieth centuries. The Church responded to the needs of immigrants by defending their dignity against xenophobia—fear or hatred of foreigners—and discrimination, advocating for their rights as workers, and providing a space for the celebration of culture in a new context.[2] The European-born immigrants who made up the majority of Catholics in the United States in the early part of the twentieth century faced suspicions that they were unpatriotic. US Catholics were divided on how to articulate that they were both Roman Catholic and American, with so-called "Romanists" advocating for parochial schools and all-Catholic associations and so-called "Americanists" supporting public schools and collaboration with Protestants in labor unions.[3] The struggles of early Catholic immigrants in the United States, although particular to that time period, highlight some of the primary issues that migrants face today—being vulnerable to exploitation of their labor, facing xenophobia and various forms of discrimination, often having to defend themselves against accusations of being un-American.

The Bishops of the United States and Mexico: *Strangers No Longer*

The Catholic Church in the United States continues to include a large immigrant population but demographics have shifted since the early twentieth century when most Catholic immigrants were from Europe. In 2010, the majority of foreign-born residents in the United States were from Mexico, followed by immigrants from South and East Asia.[4] The USCCB's response to migration reflects these demographic trends, with much of their effort focused on the issues associated with the US-Mexico border and the migration flows from Central and South America.

In 2003, the USCCB collaborated with the Catholic bishops of Mexico to write a joint pastoral letter entitled, *Strangers No Longer: Together on a Journey of Hope* (*SNL*). The letter builds on a history of CST on immigration, emphasizing the demands of the

---

2. Jay Dolan, *The American Catholic Experience: A History from Colonial Times to the Present* (Garden City, NJ: Double Day, 1985), 311–14.

3. To learn more about the tensions experienced by early Catholic immigrants to the United States, see Jay Dolan, *In Search of an American Catholicism: A History of Religion and Culture in Tension* (Oxford: Oxford University Press, 2002).

4. Pew Research Center (January 9, 2012) available online at *http://www. pewhispanic.org/2012/01/09/u-s-foreign-born-population-how-much-change-from-2009-to-2010/*.

common good and the dignity of individuals and families as criteria for evaluating the reality of immigration. This letter is notable for its message as well as its collaborative development. The USCCB and the Mexican Conference of Catholic Bishops, who lead the Catholic Church in two nations whose perspectives on migration are grounded in different contexts, jointly declared that immigration is not just about national identity or affiliation. By working together to address the issue of migration, the bishops from the United States and Mexico modeled the solidarity for which the Church has consistently advocated in debates on immigration. The bishops of the United States and Mexico both promote solidarity in their joint letter by issuing pastoral directives that will help people in both countries respond to the situation of migrants and develop public policy directives that can help governments respond justly to the reality of migration. The principles of CST, especially the call to family, community, and participation, inform the bishops' pastoral directives and policy recommendations.

The bishops' letter identifies challenges and dangers that migrants often face—economic hardship at home, unsafe passage to their destination, and lack of protection where they settle—and notes that, as a result, migrants often find themselves in unstable or dangerous situations without the assistance they need. This is especially true for undocumented migrants afraid to seek assistance or legal protection for fear that they will be detained or deported. Many undocumented migrants seek refuge in religious organizations because they are afraid of the state.[5] Churches and faith-based organizations are thus in a unique position to establish trust among migrants and are able to provide them with resources regardless of their legal status.

The bishops of the United States and Mexico recognize the position of religious organizations, including the Catholic Church, to serve immigrants in need of help and commit themselves to their pastoral care, inviting local churches to always reveal a "spirit of hospitality" toward migrants (*SNL*, no. 42). Offering hospitality involves

---

5. Margarita Mooney, "The Catholic Bishops Conferences of the United States and France: Engaging Immigration as a Public Issue," *American Behavioral Scientist* (Vol. 49: 11): 1455–70.

overcoming xenophobia and hostility toward migrants, providing resources that they need to adjust to a new culture and achieve social stability. Church leaders, in particular, should undertake the task of "the building of structures of solidarity to accompany the migrant" (*SNL*, no. 40). The bishops stress that the Christian faith mandates welcoming the migrant, asking people to see Christ in the face of the stranger and the outcast, "For I was hungry and you gave me food, I was thirsty and you gave me drink, a stranger and you welcomed me" (Matthew 25:35). Within this theological framework, responding to the migrant is part of the Church's ongoing task of conversion toward Christ. The bishops describe the implications of this:

> Part of the process of conversion of mind and heart deals with confronting attitudes of cultural superiority, indifference, and racism; accepting migrants not as foreboding aliens, terrorists, or economic threats, but rather as persons with dignity and rights, revealing the presence of Christ; and recognizing migrants as bearers of deep cultural values and rich faith traditions. (*SNL*, no. 40)

The Church calls people to see the migrant first and foremost as a person with the same dignity and rights as all others and to serve the needs of immigrants without legal status-based discrimination.

Many migrants have chosen to leave family members behind in order to come to the United States to work and send money home. In 2005 immigrants sent an estimated $233 billion US dollars to family in their country of origin.[6] This money supports international development when wealthier countries fail to provide such funds through international aid or enact unjust trade policies that disadvantage impoverished countries. Ultimately, the lack of international solidarity perpetuates economically driven migration and leads to the separation of families. This is problematic in light of the principle of the call to family, community, and participation because it ignores the demands of the global common good, and it undermines the basic social structure of the family. The reunification of families is a top priority for the bishops of

---

6. Mary DeLory, "International Migration: Social, Economic, and Humanitarian Considerations," in Donald Kerwin and Jill Marie Geschutz, *And You Welcomed Me: Migration and Catholic Social Teaching* (Lanham, MD: Lexington Books, 2009), 43.

Catholic Social Teaching on Migration Rights

CST has insisted on the right to migrate since Pope Pius XII's *Exsul familia Nazarethana* (*The Exiled Family from Nazareth,* 1952). The Catholic Church's teaching, however, has also called for the investigation of the root causes of migration and the creation of conditions that will eliminate migration that is forced by economic hardship. CST has consistently challenged unrestricted liberal capitalism that exacerbates the gap between wealthy and poor nations. In *Populorum progressio* (*The Development of Peoples,* 1967) Pope Paul VI criticized a type of tyranny that results when profits and free competition are the guiding norms of economics (no. 26). The disparity of wealth among nations, supported by unfair trade agreements that favor wealthier nations and multinational corporations, creates the conditions in which citizens of less developed countries, desperate to gain financial security, often feel compelled by necessity to migrate. Critiquing this reality, the US and Mexican bishops suggest that "this is the ideal situation for which the world and both countries should strive: one in which migration flows are driven by choice, not necessity" (*SNL,* no. 59).

the United States and Mexico. They critique immigration policies that weaken family unity and argue that the situation encourages undocumented immigration. The bishops argue that "a new framework must be established that will give Mexican families more opportunities to legally reunite with their loved ones in the United States" (*SNL,* no. 66).

The same economic forces that motivate migrants to leave their families in Mexico provide jobs in the United States. The reality is that immigrants (documented and undocumented) respond to a high demand in the US job market, working in jobs that many Americans do not want. Immigrants often work in construction, agriculture, and the service industry—traditionally, low-paying and labor-intensive jobs. Furthermore, the demand of US consumers for cheap goods and services (especially when this demand is unmet by strong advocacy for labor) creates an economy that is dependent on low-wage workers. The bishops, among others, argue that because the US economy has created the demand for migrant labor, it needs to make provisions for safe and fair participation in the economy. The bishops state, "the United States needs Mexican laborers to maintain a healthy economy and should make a special effort to provide legal avenues for Mexican workers to obtain in the United States jobs that provide a living wage and appropriate benefits and labor protections" (*SNL*, no. 72). The bishops continue the Catholic social tradition's insistence on the rights of workers, which is grounded in the dignity of the human person and the dignity of work. These rights, which include a just wage, safe working conditions, and nondiscrimination in the workplace, transcend the legal status of an individual. The bishops defend the dignity of documented and undocumented workers while advocating for pathways to legalization of migrant workers in the United States. They state, "We recognize that, as an alternative to undocumented migration, an efficient legal pathway must be established that protects the basic labor rights of foreign-born workers" (*SNL*, no. 75). Specifically, they suggest that the United States needs to provide a greater number of both temporary and permanent worker visas to prevent the abuse of undocumented migrant workers (*SNL*, no. 72).

The principle of human dignity is at the heart of the bishops' response to migration. The bishops echo Pope John Paul II's unconditional defense of the dignity of the migrant. In his address on World Migration Day, he stated that "his [the migrant's] irregular legal status cannot allow the migrant to lose his dignity, since he is endowed with inalienable rights."[7] In other words, human rights must be protected regardless of one's legal status. This does not mean that the Catholic Church supports illegal immigration. In fact, the Catholic social tradition explicitly supports the right and responsibility of a nation to control its borders. However, the way that it controls its borders cannot violate the dignity of each person or the disregard the global common good. *Strangers No Longer* states,

---

7. John Paul II, "Undocumented Migrants," no. 2, 1996 World Migration Day Address, available online at *http://www.vatican.va/holy_father/john_paul_ii/messages/migration/documents/hf_jp-ii_mes_25071995_undocumented_migrants_en.html*.

The Catholic Church recognizes the right and responsibility of sovereign nations to control their borders and to ensure the security interests of their citizens. Therefore, we accept the legitimate role of the U.S. and Mexican governments in intercepting undocumented migrants who attempt to travel through or cross into one of the two countries. We do not accept, however, some of the policies and tactics that our governments have employed to meet this shared responsibility. (No. 78)

Using the principle of human dignity, the bishops critique some of the tactics practiced in the detainment centers on the US-Mexico border. The bishops offer examples of inhumane treatment, citing

The Kino Border Initiative

A number of religious and nonreligious organizations have responded to the need for humanitarian relief at the US-Mexico border. For example, the Kino Border Initiative (KBI) brings together the resources of the Catholic community to minister to migrants on both sides of the US-Mexico border. Sponsored by the California Province of Jesuits, the Catholic Diocese of Tucson, the Mexico Province of Jesuits, the Missionary Sisters of the Eucharist, the Jesuit Refugee Service/USA, and the Archdiocese of Hermosillo, KBI coordinates services near the border for recently deported migrants. The services include the provision of meals, first aid, and shelter. KBI also promotes education about migration by sponsoring immersion programs for high school and university students, allowing them to observe the reality of migration at the border. By focusing on collaboration among parishes on both sides of the US-Mexico border, KBI promotes solidarity and provides a visible expression of the Christian discipleship transcending national borders to defend human dignity and enhance the common good. See Web site: *www.kinoborderinitiative.org*.

"documented abuses of migrants," the use of "excessive force" to detain migrants, and the use of "dilapidated detention facilities" to contain unaccompanied minors (*SNL*, nos. 80–82). The border initiatives employed to deter illegal immigration have proved to be largely ineffective, only driving migrants to pursue dangerous routes, as in the case of the popular Sonora Desert route. The number of migrant deaths has doubled since 1994 when the United States began enforcing more stringent border patrol at known crossing points.[8] Drawing on the principle of human dignity, the bishops issue a defense of the sanctity of life and challenge the United States and Mexico to control their borders in a way that minimizes death and assists "migrants in distress" (*SNL*, no. 89).

Reading the Signs of the Times: Undocumented Immigrants in the United States

The context of migration is always shifting, making ongoing social analysis necessary. Because immigration is such an important political topic in the United States today, one is challenged continually to evaluate policies and proposals for immigration reform. This section will illustrate a small piece of a much larger and complex reality, focusing on the issue of undocumented migrants in the United States today. By highlighting the strong economic factors behind illegal migration to the United States and briefly outlining the limited pathways to legal migration, this section sets up an ethical dilemma. Describing the work of Catholic theologian Daniel Groody on the topic demonstrates how the Catholic social tradition can inform the issue of migration.

Migration to the United States is largely influenced by economic factors shaped by the international community. The 2009 United Nations Human Development Report reveals a strong connection

---

8. US Government Accountability Office, *Illegal Immigration: Border Crossing Deaths Have Doubled Since 1995; Border Patrol's Efforts to Prevent Deaths Have Not Been Fully Evaluated*, GAO-06-770 (Washington, DC: US Government Accountability Office, August 2006), 16; as cited in Donald Kerwin, "Rights, the Common Good and Sovereignty," in Kerwin and Geschutz, *And You Welcomed Me*, 113.

between migration and the pursuit of opportunities to develop as people and improve life for their families. The report indicates that the majority of international migrants travel from an underdeveloped country to a more economically developed country.[9] Mexico, the country of origin for most of the US foreign-born population, has a per capita Gross National Income rate of $8,920 as compared to the US $47,240.[10] The growing economic disparity between wealthy and poor nations undoubtedly fuels increased migration. Today, almost half of the world's population lives on less than two US dollars a day, and around 550 million people live on less than one US dollar per day.[11] This reality makes US wages attractive, even if workers are making less than the 2009 legal minimum of $7.25 per hour. Examining the reality of immigration in light of the global economy highlights the connection between human development and migration flows.

Opportunities for legal migration to the United States are limited. The US Department of Homeland Security lists four broad categories designating pathways for non-US citizens to achieve legal permanent resident (LPR) status. These categories are presented from the greatest number granted in 2009 to the least: (1) family sponsorship (which includes children, spouses, and parents of US citizens), (2) employer-based sponsorship preference, (3) refugees and asylees preference, and (4) diversity preference (allowing immigrants of countries that have low migration flows to the United States).[12] The majority of family sponsorships were given to spouses of US citizens followed by parents and children of US citizens.[13] Even these sponsorships are difficult and costly to obtain. For example, an immigrant from Mexico, whose natural citizens accounted for the greatest number of LPRs in

9. UN Human Development Report 2009 available online at *http://hdr.undp.org/en/media/HDR_2009_EN_Overview.pdf*.

10. Data on GNI provided by the World Bank available at *http://data.worldbank.org/indicator/NY.GNP.PCAP.CD*.

11. Global Commission on International Migration 2005 Report, 11.

12. US Department of Homeland Security 2009 Report on US Legal Permanent Residents *http://www.dhs.gov/xlibrary/assets/statistics/publications/lpr_fr_2009.pdf*

13. Ibid.

2009,[14] would be considered ineligible for the diversity preference. Employer-based preferences are highly sought after but limited in number, accounting for only 12.7 percent of the LPRs in 2009.[15] Out of that 12.7 percent, the majority were professionals with an advanced degree or skilled workers in a sector identified as a priority area for the US economy.[16]

The majority of undocumented workers seeking permanent resident status in the United States are less-skilled workers without college degrees. Although the data show how difficult it is for these individuals to obtain legal status, they fulfill a strong demand in the US job market. As demographics of developed countries shift toward an aging population with lower birthrates, the need for unskilled laborers increases. Without a population willing to take low-income, less-skilled jobs, there is a high demand for migrant workers. The US immigration policy, however, does not reflect these demographic and economic shifts, offering the majority of employer-based preferences to highly educated professionals with specialized skills. US lawyers John Hoeffner and Michele Pistone conclude that "in particular, a discrepancy exists between the strength of forces propelling migrants into the United States and the ability of current law to recognize in some official way the reality of their presence. Hence, the problem of the undocumented immigrant."[17]

The problem of the undocumented immigrant can be examined from the perspectives of many different people—politicians, immigration lawyers, business owners and employees, and the millions people that pursue international migration each year.[18] Catholic priest and scholar Daniel Groody examines migration from a theological perspective, emphasizing the Christian belief that the human person reflects the image and likeness of God. On this basis, he

---

14. Ibid.

15. Ibid.

16.. Ibid.

17. John Hoeffner and Michele Pistone, "But the Laborers Are . . . Many: Catholic Social Teaching on Business, Labor, and Economic Migration." in Kerwin and Geschutz, *And You Welcomed Me*, 69.

18. The UN Human Development Report estimates that two-hundred million people pursued international migration in 2009. See *http://hdr.undp.org/en/media/HDR_2009_EN_Overview.pdf*.

challenges some of the language used to categorize migrants such as *aliens* and *illegal*. Such language can obscure the humanity of migrants and promote attitudes and policies that undermine their human rights. Furthermore, categories fail to identify adequately the economic injustices motivating migration flows. Groody suggests "categories such as legality and illegality, the documented and the undocumented, and citizen and alien, not only fail to come to terms with a new global reality, but they also leave gaping areas of injustice in their wake."[19] Emphasizing the humanity of migrants has moral implications, mandating policies that honor the rights of migrants and protect their dignity.

Summary and Integration for Service Learners

This chapter explored some ethical dimensions of migration with a focus on migration from Mexico to the United States. The Catholic Church has responded to the immediate needs of migrants, many of whom lack social and legal support. Recognizing the situation of these migrants, the USCCB and Mexican bishops have challenged the churches to be a place of refuge and help for migrants, providing hospitality and assistance. The Catholic Church in the United States has also engaged in advocacy for just immigration reform guided by the priorities of protecting the rights and dignity of migrants. Their advocacy also focuses on promoting economic justice that allows everyone to participate in the international common good and on defending the unity of the family.

These guidelines are rooted in the Christian theological tradition, which insists that people are social beings, created in the image of a relational God and created for community with others. The call to family, community, and participation is rooted in this theology and has developed as a foundational principle of CST. The issues surrounding migration highlight the importance of this principle as it challenges people to promote solidarity in the international

---

19. Daniel Groody, "Crossing the Divide: Foundations of a Theology of Migration and Refugees," *Theological Studies*, Vol. 70 (2000): 639.

community, create pathways for participation in society among the marginalized, and protect the dignity of the family.

Having learned about some ethical dimensions of migration, revisit your responses to the questions in the introduction. Has the chapter led you to rethink any of your answers? Has it confirmed any of your assumptions about the meaning of community or the importance of family? How does the principle of the call to family, community, and participation inform your attitudes about migrants? Use the following vignette and questions to practice the see-judge-act process in relation to this topic.

Meeting an Immigrant

Service-Learning Vignette

A service learner working as a translator in a free health clinic for women spent an afternoon hearing one woman's story of migrating to the United States. Originally from a small town in Oaxaca, Mexico, the woman decided to come to the United States three years ago because she needed a job to support her aging parents. She used her entire savings to hire a guide to cross the US-Mexico border and to pay for a bus ticket to San Francisco, where she could live with relatives. She now works as a housekeeper for a woman she met at church. She told the student that she would like to go to school to become a teacher but she cannot afford it because she only makes $3.50 an hour and she tries to send home as much money as possible. She also told the student that she misses her parents terribly but is afraid that if she went home to visit, she would not make it back across the border. She thinks that the best thing she can do for her family members right now is to keep sending them money.

See: Social Analysis

- What social, political, and economic factors may have contributed to the woman's decision to migrate? Can you identify any social injustices that may have led to her migration?
- Consider the obstacles preventing the woman from finding sustainable work and being with her family. How many of these

factors can be attributed to her decisions? What factors are beyond her control?

Judge: Ethical Reflection

- Consider the woman's situation in light of the principle of the call to community. What priorities emerge? When you consider the implications of this principle, do you see the woman's situation differently?
- Evaluate Groody's challenge to some of the language used to categorize migrants in light of CST. Can you identify language that better reflects the migrants' dignity?

Act: Promoting Justice

- Based on what you have learned about CST and some of the challenges surrounding migration in the United States today, what do you think should be done to address the issue of undocumented migration?
- Identify immediate and long-term actions aligned with CST that respond to the situation of undocumented immigrants. What is the role of faith communities, nonprofit organizations, and the government in taking these actions?

Suggestions for Further Social Analysis in a Service-Learning Context

- What services are available for immigrants in a selected city or service-learning context? How are these services promoted and accessed? What services can immigrants obtain without documentation?
- Research data on migration flows into a selected city, and identify any patterns. What political and economic factors might be motivating these migration patterns?
- Research the immigration enforcement policies and practices of a selected state. How do these relate to federal policies? What are some of the current debates behind state and federal policies?

For Further Reading on Catholic Social Thought and Migration

Cruz, Gemma Tulud. "Toward an Ethic of Risk: Catholic Social Teaching and Immigration Reform." *Studies in Christian Ethics*, Vol. 24, issue 3 (August 2011): 294–310.

De la Torre, Miguel. *Trials of Hope and Terror: Testimonies on Immigration.* Maryknoll, NY: Orbis Press, 2009.

Groody, Daniel. *A Promised Land, a Perilous Journey: Theological Perspectives on Migration.* Notre Dame, IN: University of Notre Dame Press, 2008.

Heyer, Kristin. *Kinship across Borders: A Christian Ethic of Migration.* Washington, DC: Georgetown University Press, 2012.

Kerwin, Donald, and Jill Marie Geschutz. *And You Welcomed Me: Migration and Catholic Social Teaching.* Lanham, MD: Lexington Books, 2009.

chapter 4

Justice for Workers and the Dignity of Work

Introduction

Protecting the dignity of work is a fundamental principle of Catholic social teaching (CST). The topic of work is prominent in many of the major social encyclicals, including Pope Leo XIII's *Rerum novarum* (*On the Condition of Labor*, 1891), which addressed the ethical dimensions of work in the context of the Industrial Revolution and has continued to be an important theme in CST. Reflect on your understanding of the meaning of work and its moral dimensions using the following questions:

- What is the meaning and purpose of work? Does your understanding of work include unpaid work? Does it include service learning?
- What is your experience of work? Have any work experiences of your own raised justice-related concerns? If so, explain. What are your hopes for work in the future? What, if anything, might stand in the way of you realizing your hopes?
- How do you understand the Catholic Church's call to protect the dignity of work? How is the dignity of work realized? What signs might indicate that the dignity of work is not being protected?

The unjust treatment of workers is a sign that community is failing to protect the dignity of work. Signs of injustice can take on many forms, including long-term unemployment, insufficient wages, and exploitation in the workplace. Consider what you already know about the violation of workers' rights.

- What rights do workers have? Who is responsible for enforcing rules that protect these rights?
- Is work a concern among people you may have met in a service-learning context? If so, what are their concerns? How do these people's hopes about work compare with your hopes for work?
- What conditions, practices, and policies create security for workers? What conditions, practices, and policies make workers vulnerable?

This chapter will address the topic of work by highlighting major developments in CST on the dignity of work and rights of workers. It will examine teachings about work in the early social encyclicals, focusing on *Rerum novarum*, highlight the connection between work and integral human development in the writings of Pope Paul VI and review John Paul II's personalist approach to work in *Laborem exercens* (*On Human Work*, 1981). Then the chapter will examine some ways the United States Conference of Catholic Bishops (USCCB) have applied the principle of the dignity of work to labor issues in the United States. Next, the chapter will present information that can inform social analysis about vulnerable workers in the United States today. The final section of the chapter provides a summary followed by a vignette drawn from an actual service-learning setting and a series of questions designed to help readers practice aspects of the see-judge-act process.

The Dignity of Work in Catholic Social Teaching

Labor in the Early Social Encyclicals

The first social encyclical, *Rerum novarum* (*On the Condition of Labor*), focuses on ethical questions raised in the aftermath of the Industrial Revolution, which began in Europe in the late eighteenth century and later spread to other countries including the United States. The nature and context of work had shifted significantly with new forms of production that supported the economic system of capitalism. Factories were able to manufacture a surplus of goods, and owners of raw materials employed workers to turn those materials into products. However, without the government regulations that many people rely on today to ensure that workers are treated with fairness and dignity, employers could legally exploit workers in order to maximize profits. As a result, industrial workers endured long hours, often without breaks or weekends, and they often worked in unhealthy or dangerous conditions for poor wages. This new situation raised questions about workers and the conditions of their work.

In *Rerum novarum*, Pope Leo XIII denounced the competitive and individualistic spirit of capitalism that drove employers to exploit workers, and he rejected the utopian vision of equality that socialists offered as an alternative to capitalism. The pope argued that natural inequalities necessarily exist in social life and that people should treat each other with dignity but not expect that inequalities be leveled (*RN*, no. 17). Against the socialists, Leo XIII defended the worker's natural right to private property and rejected intervention from the state that would violate this right. At the same time, the pope argued that the state has a role in protecting the natural rights of workers, such as the right to private property and the right to wages that are sufficient for supporting a family (*RN*, nos. 30–34). This understanding of the government's role in economic life is at the core of the Catholic Church's current support of living wage laws and regulations.

Leo XIII was also concerned that socialists would undermine the moral authority of the Catholic Church. The pope did not want to lose the working class to the promise of hope the socialists offered workers. In *Rerum novarum*, Leo XIII invites people to look to the Catholic Church and the Christian faith for meaning in their suffering. Thus, he offers a theological interpretation of the suffering associated with work, suggesting that it is a result of the fall recounted in the book of Genesis (3:17–19). Leo XIII suggests,

> As regards bodily labor, even had man never fallen from the state of innocence, he would not have remained wholly idle; but that which would then have been his free choice and his delight became afterwards compulsory, and the painful expiation for his disobedience. "Cursed be the earth in thy work; in thy labor thou shalt eat of it all the days of thy life." (*RN*, no. 17)

Minimum Wage vs. Living Wage

Catholic social thought advocates for a living wage because current minimum wage laws do not necessarily prevent families from living in poverty. Based on the 2012 federal minimum wage of $7.25 per hour, a full-time worker earns about $15,000 per year.[1] The 2010 United States Census Bureau identifies the poverty threshold for a family consisting of two adults and one child at $15,030.[2] The principle behind the argument for a living wage is that people who are earning wages for full-time employment should not have to live in poverty. Living wages are based on estimates of the cost of living in particular areas. The state of California, for example, had a minimum wage of $8.00 per hour in 2012, but experts estimated that the living wage, for a family of two adults and one child, in California at that time was $20.80 per hour.[3]

The pope connects the suffering of workers to human sinfulness. Subsequent developments of CST point out two time-bound limitations of Leo XIII's understanding of work. First, locating the suffering of human labor in the fall does not promote a structural analysis of economic injustices that perpetuate the suffering of workers. Second, it does not capture the positive aspect of work as an expression of human subjectivity. By focusing on the person doing the work rather than the work itself, work can be understood as the way that people express themselves as individuals and participate in the social life of a community.

---

1. Kai Filion, "Minimum Wage Anniversary: Still Helping Millions of Workers Get By, but Just Barely," Economic Policy Institute (July 23, 2010) available at *http://www.epi.org/publication/minimum_wage_anniversary_still_helping_millions_of_workers_get_by_but_/*.

2. The United States Census Bureau, Poverty Data for 2010 available at *http://www.census.gov/hhes/www/poverty/data/threshld/index.html.*

3. According to the Massachusetts Institute of Technology (MIT) Living Wage Calculator available online at *http://livingwage.mit.edu.*

The Catholic social tradition is marked by continuity with and development of Leo XIII's thoughts on labor. The tradition has consistently supported the dignity of work, the provision a living wage so the worker can support a family and maintain private property, and the value of labor unions in protecting the rights of workers and promoting cooperation in the labor market. Two developments since *Rerum novarum* are particularly notable. First, Pope Paul VI's approach to integral human development, which locates the aspiration for freedom and equality in the nature of the human person, challenged Leo XIII's assumption that natural inequalities exist. Second, John Paul II's development of a personalist approach to work, which emphasized the positive value of work as an expression of the individual and the way that an individual participates in community, nuanced Leo XIII's linking of work and suffering as part of the lot of fallen humanity.

Pope Paul VI: Human Development and Work

During the Second Vatican Council, Pope Paul VI attended to developing countries and human development. At this time the United Nations was raising awareness about the effects of colonization and global inequalities.[4] Paul VI also wanted to raise awareness about the shocking disparity between rich and poor countries. His focus, however, went beyond the rich and poor disparity to include what he described as integral human development. Two years after the close of the council, Paul VI wrote his encyclical letter *Populorum progressio* (*The Development of Peoples*, 1967). In *Populorum progressio* (*PP*), the pope described human development as follows:

> The development we speak of here cannot be restricted to economic growth alone. To be authentic, it must be well rounded; it must foster the development of each man and of the whole man. . . . Self-development, however, is not left up to man's option. Just as the whole of creation is ordered toward its Creator, so too the rational creature should of his own accord direct his life to God, the first truth and

---

4. Marvin Mich, *Catholic Social Teaching and Movements* (Mystic, CT: Twenty-Third Publications, 2006), 155–57.

the highest good. Thus human self-fulfillment may be said to sum up our obligations. Moreover, this harmonious integration of our human nature, carried through by personal effort and responsible activity, is destined for a higher state of perfection. United with the life-giving Christ, man's life is newly enhanced; it acquires a transcendent humanism which surpasses its nature and bestows new fullness of life. This is the highest goal of human self-fulfillment. (Nos. 14, 16)

In Paul VI's view, the aspiration to the fullness of life is an innate part of the human person, an expression of one's dignity and willed by God. Social structures that thwart the human drive toward conditions that support the fullness of life can lead to social conflict and even violent revolutions (*PP*, no. 30). By acknowledging the possibility of violence, Paul VI is not condoning revolutionary violence, but he is expressing more sympathy toward revolutionary movements than Leo XIII did in 1891. Paul VI follows his immediate predecessor, Pope John XXIII, in affirming that justice and the protection of human rights are the foundations of peace. This perspective is grounded in the observation that social inequalities inhibit lasting peace. Paul VI's emphasis on integral human development and the transformation of unjust structures challenges the notion that natural inequalities exist. His perspective locates injustices in the dynamics of human history rather than unchanging features of human nature. The thought of Paul VI lays the foundation for workers to expect justice so that they can, through their work, achieve self-fulfillment.

Pope John Paul II: A Personalist Approach to Labor

On the ninetieth anniversary of *Rerum novarum* (*On the Condition of Labor*), Pope John Paul II issued a social encyclical on human work, *Laborem exercens* (*On Human Work*). Many people consider this encyclical to be one of the greatest contributions to the Catholic Church's social teaching on work. [5] It exemplifies John Paul II's

---

5. On the reactions to *Laborem exercens*, see Patricia Lamoureux, "Commentary on *Laborem exercens* (*On Human Work*)" in *Modern Catholic Social Teaching: Commentaries and Interpretations,* ed. Kenneth Himes, et al. (Washington, DC: Georgetown University Press, 2005), 408–10.

personalist worldview, which locates the human person at the center of reality and judges reality based on how it conforms to the conviction that all people have inherent dignity. Within a personalist perspective, the human person must never be a marginal concern but is rather the central concern of decisions and actions.[6] Personalism stresses that the human person must never be an object, something to be acted on but must always be the subject of social life, with agency, dignity, and freedom.

By rejecting all thought and action that objectifies people, personalism adds an important dimension to the Catholic Church's understanding of work. The *Compendium of the Social Doctrine of the Church* (2004) summarizes this dimension by saying that "*all of social life is an expression of its unmistakable protagonist: the human person*" (no. 106).[7] In other words, the people are the center of social life, the main characters in history as it unfolds. The specifically Christian understanding of personalism, which John Paul II developed, views and evaluates reality through the lens of a theological understanding of the human person: the human person is created in the image and likeness of God, redeemed by God, and destined for union with God at the end of time.

This perspective shapes John Paul II's understanding of work in several ways. First, he insists in *Laborem exercens* (*LE*) that the human person is and must always be treated as the subject of work. He states: "As *a person, man is therefore the subject of work*. As a person he works, he performs various actions belonging to the work process; independently of their objective content, these actions must all serve to realize his humanity, to fulfill the calling to be a person that is his by reason of his very humanity" (*LE*, no. 6). In other words, the value of the person is never determined by the kind of work he or she performs. The product of work can never be valued above the person and the person can never be considered alongside the other means of productivity. Within a personalist perspective on work, there is a fundamental difference between a person and a machine, a person and a material,

---

6. Bernard Brady, *Essential Catholic Social Thought* (Maryknoll, NY: Orbis, 2008), 32–36.

7. Pontifical Council for Justice and Peace, *The Compendium of the Social Doctrine of the Church* (Libreria Editrice Vaticana, 2004).

a person and a profit. For the pope, the person must always be the primary concern and should never be treated as a means to an end.

John Paul II grounds work in the subjectivity of the human person by referring to the book of Genesis, which invites people to "fill the earth and subdue it" (1:28). He interprets this passage to mean that the impulse to work is grounded in and unique to human nature. This impulse is seen as God's invitation to participate in creation, contribute to social life, and express one's unique dignity. As such, work should not just be something that a person endures for the sake of survival. Even though many people have to work in jobs that they experience as obligatory and meaningless, the fundamental meaning of work is tied to the nature of the human person. Work is an expression of the human person: "Work is a good thing for man—a good thing for his humanity—because through work man *not only transforms nature*, adapting it to his own needs, but he also *achieves fulfillment* as a human being and indeed, in a sense, becomes 'more a human being'" (*LE*, no. 9).

John Paul II's personalist understanding of work highlights that work is a human activity with moral significance and a positive expression of the worker as a person. If one considers work to be an expression of human subjectivity, then work is personal. Considering the personal dimension of work can help one understand why people often express anger when someone takes credit for their work. It can also help explain why people can become depressed when they can no longer work. Work is also social. Work allows people to participate in their family, community, and larger society. Within the framework offered by John Paul II, the way that individuals define their work, relate to workers, and structure their lives around work all carries moral significance.

The United States Conference of Catholic Bishops on Labor

CST's call to defend the dignity of work and the rights of workers has practical implications for approaching work-related issues such as labor unions, wages, working conditions, and employment. The USCCB has applied CST to particular issues affecting US workers. This section will present a brief discussion of the role of Catholics in the early labor movement and an overview of the themes of the USCCB's recent Labor Day statements.

The Early Labor Movement

The early labor movement in the United States relied heavily on Catholic participation. In the late 1800s and early 1900s, Catholic immigrants from Ireland, Italy, and Germany made up a large portion of the labor market. Like many immigrants today, the immigrants of this era tended to work in jobs that made them vulnerable to insufficient wages, unsafe working conditions, and long workdays. Labor unions developed to give workers a voice to advocate for fairness in the workplace. Lay Catholics were instrumental in the development of one of the first labor unions in the United States, the Knights of Labor, in 1869. Despite strong participation among laypeople, the Catholic hierarchy was divided over whether or not to support the Knights of Labor largely because of internal debates within the Catholic Church on how the Church should express itself as a religious minority in a predominantly Protestant country. Some bishops argued that Catholics should participate in the public life of American society by sending their kids to public schools and interacting with non-Catholics. Others encouraged Catholics to support Catholic schools and avoid socializing with non-Catholics. The question at the heart of the debate was how to assimilate into American life and maintain Catholic identity, which was also tied to their cultural identity as immigrants.[8] "Some of the hierarchy opposed the Knights of Labor out of fear that labor unions promoted secrecy, anarchy, and socialism."[9] At stake in this debate was the pastoral question of how to serve a Catholic immigrant population that was working class and a religious minority in the United States. Also at stake was the question of how to interpret and apply the Church's emerging social teaching in a non-European context.

---

8. For a historical analysis of this period, see Jay Dolan, *The American Catholic Experience: A History from Colonial Times to the Present* (Notre Dame, IN: The University of Notre Dame Press, 1992).

9. John O'Brien, *George Higgins and the Quest for Worker Justice: The Evolution of Catholic Social Thought in America* (Lanham, MD: Rowman & Littlefield Publishers, 2005), 29–30.

Though Catholics in Europe had different concerns than Catholics of the United States, many of the teachings in *Rerum novarum* were applicable in the United States, particularly its defense of the rights of workers. Ultimately, US Cardinal James Gibbons was able in 1887 to convince the Vatican officially to support the Knights of Labor by drawing on the Catholic Church's social teaching. He quoted *Rerum novarum* to convince the pope that labor unions had an important role in society by giving a voice to workers. This had lasting implications in the development of the Catholic social tradition in the United States. Catholic historian John O'Brien notes, "Once the Vatican lifted the ban on the Knights, the church was perceived as being officially on the side of labor."[10]

Labor Priests in the United States

The Catholic Church's support of labor was exemplified in the early 1900s by labor priests. Labor priests were leading advocates for the rights of workers, supporting strikes and boycotts and providing encouragement to workers using the principles of *Rerum novarum* (*On the Condition of Labor*).[11] For example, Peter Yorke, a Catholic priest from San Francisco, supported workers through his writings and activism. He helped organize strikes among dockworkers as well as cable-car workers who were fighting for fair wages and reasonable work hours.[12]

John Ryan, a labor priest and scholar who influenced the US bishops, applied CST to labor issues in the United States. Ryan, a professor at the Catholic University of America, taught and wrote about economic justice in the aftermath of World War I. Specifically, he used CST to advocate for a living wage, federal and state laws

---

10. Ibid., 32.
11. Ibid., 40–56.
12. Ibid., 46.

designed to protect workers, and the development of labor unions to strengthen the decision-making power of workers.[13]

The US bishops officially addressed some labor and economic issues in the United States in their 1919 document, *Bishops' Program of Social Reconstruction*.[14] In this document the bishops echoed much of Ryan's thought, advocating for the workers' right to organize and receive just wages from their employers. In addition, the bishops argued that the government is responsible for protecting the rights of workers. The *Program of Social Reconstruction* reflects a shift in the US Catholic bishops' stance on labor. Within a few decades, the bishops had gone from being divided on whether to support unions to supporting organized labor, living wages, child labor laws, and social welfare systems.[15]

The United States Conference of Catholic Bishops' Recent Labor Day Statements

Today, the USCCB continues to speak on labor and the economy. One way they do this is by issuing a "Labor Day Statement" each year that draws on the same principles of CST that influenced the early Catholic labor priests to address contemporary situations.

The 2009 Labor Day statement, for example, draws on Pope Benedict XVI's social encyclical, *Caritas in veritate* (*Charity in Truth*, 2009), which identifies work as an expression of workers' dignity and creativity, allowing them to reflect the image and likeness of God in the world. The 2009 statement points out an implication of this theological understanding of work, suggesting that the "vision of cooperation with God in building up this world through our work underscores the need for us all to cooperate and collaborate with one another in making work and the workplace a project of human solidarity and mutual respect."[16]

---

13. Mary Elsbernd, "Work and Workers in the Pastoral Letters of the United States Conference of Bishops," *Louvain Studies* Vol. 19 (1994): 222–24.

14. *Bishops' Program of Social Reconstruction* [reprint], Washington, DC: National Catholic Welfare Conference, 1950.

15. For a historical account of this era, see Elsbernd, "Work and Workers."

16. Bishop William F. Murphy, Chairman of the Committee on Domestic Justice and Human Development USCCB, "Labor Day Statement: The Value of Work; The Dignity of the Human Person" (September 7, 2009) *http://old.usccb.org/sdwp/national/labor_day_2009.pdf*.

The 2010 and 2011 Labor Day statements focus on the issue of widespread unemployment and poverty in the context of an economic recession. In the 2011 statement, the bishops remind readers that these issues "are not just economic, but also ethical. They are not just institutional, but also personal."[17] Drawing on the social teaching of the Catholic Church, the bishops offer principles to guide ethical responses to the labor issues that pay particular attention to how these issues impact people. They emphasize the need to work together to alleviate unemployment and to promote policies that reflect a preferential option for the poor and vulnerable.

In the 2011 Labor Day statement, the bishops also discuss the Catholic Church's position on labor unions, stating,

> Beginning in *Rerum novarum*, the Church has consistently supported efforts of workers to join together to defend their rights and protect their dignity. . . . Without endorsing every tactic of unions or every outcome of collective bargaining, the Church affirms the rights of workers in public and private employment to choose to come together to form and join unions, to bargain collectively, and to have an effective voice in the workplace.[18]

The bishops' affirmation of CST's support of labor unions is significant in light of contemporary debates about the role of labor unions in the United States economy. The strong Catholic support of labor unions in the early part of the twentieth century weakened as Catholics moved out into the middle and upper classes in the second half of the twentieth century.[19] The bishops remind their audience that, even as contexts change, the Church's support of workers' rights, including the right to form unions, has been consistent.

---

17. Bishop Stephen Blaire, Chairman of the Committee on Domestic Justice and Human Development, USCCB, "Labor Day Statement: Human Costs and Moral Challenges of a Broken Economy" (September 5, 2011) *http://www.usccb.org/about/domestic-social-development/upload/Labor-Day-2011.pdf.*

18. Ibid.

19. Kristen Hannum, "Labor Pains" *US Catholic*, Vol. 76, Issue 8 (August 2011): 12–17. Hannum cites findings by the Pew Research Forum indicating that 48 percent of Catholics and 42 percent of Protestants view unions favorably.

Reading the Signs of the Times: Vulnerable Workers

This section will further consider the rights of workers by presenting information about vulnerable workers in the United States—information that contributes to the social analysis one might do when following the see-judge-act process to plan action that responds to work-related injustices.

The economic recession of 2008 affected employment rates, wages, and job security in the United States. At its height, 9.5 percent of the population was unemployed, and there was one job opening for every 4.7 people looking for work.[20] Although this statistic should be enough to invite serious ethical reflection on the economy, it does not capture the extent to which people, especially children, are affected by joblessness in the United States. In 2010, thirteen million children were living with an unemployed or underemployed parent. This is up from 6.4 million children in 2007.[21] Behind these numbers are actual people, many of whom earnestly seek work and may experience the harmful psychological effects of long-term unemployment, such as increased depression and anxiety.[22]

Unemployment in an area, especially when it occurs at a high rate or tends to be long term, can lead to an increase in the numbers of workers considered vulnerable, those who are particularly susceptible to insufficient wages, unsafe working conditions, and exploitation from employers. Workers with jobs that do not require specialized training, also described as low-skilled jobs, are more likely to be mistreated than those with jobs that require specialized training. Industries with many such low-skilled workers include the restaurant and hospitality industries, construction, manufacturing, and agriculture.[23]

---

20. Economic Policy Institute, "Labor Day by the Numbers" available at *http://www.epi.org/publication/labor-day-by-the-numbers-2011/*.

21. Lawrence Mishel, "Share of Children with at Least One Unemployed or Underemployed Parent," Economic Policy Institute (September 8, 2011) available at *http://www.epi.org/publication/share-children-unemployed-underemployed/*.

22. Paul Karsten and Moser Klaus, "Unemployment Impairs Mental Health: Meta-Analyses" *Journal of Vocational Behavior*, Vol. 74, no. 3 (June 2009): 264–82.

23. See David Wiel, "Rethinking the Regulation of Vulnerable Work in the USA: A Sector-Based Approach," *Journal of Industrial Relations*, Vol. 51, Issue 3 (June 2009): 411–30.

The Rights of Agricultural Workers

The USCCB addressed the ethical dimensions of agricultural work in their 2003 pastoral letter, *"For I Was Hungry and You Gave Me Food: Catholic Reflections on Food, Farmers, and Farmworkers."* They draw on the Catholic social tradition's framework for economic justice, stating, "We believe that the economy, including the agricultural economy, must serve people, not the other way around. . . . Employers are obligated to treat their workers with dignity, providing decent wages, safe working conditions, and humane living conditions."

Among the many workers in low-skilled jobs, farmworkers are particularly at risk for exploitation due to the laws and the effects of immigration status. The federal Fair Labor Standards Act sets different policies for farmworkers than for other sectors of the workforce and does not necessarily address conditions unique to agricultural work.[24] Specifically, employers are not required to ensure safety from the heat, leaving farmworkers vulnerable to heat exhaustion and other heat-related health issues. Federal child labor laws aim to protect young workers, but the rules for the agricultural sector of the workforce do not provide the same protections as for other sectors. Children as young as twelve can do farm work as long as it is outside of school hours and their parents give consent.[25] The immigration status of many agricultural workers makes them more vulnerable to exploitation on the job as they are afraid to seek legal protection of their rights. The majority of agricultural jobs are held by people born outside of the

---

24. The Fair Labor Standards Act (FLSA) regulates the minimum wage, youth employment, hours worked per week, and overtime within the United States. Many states have additional regulations for these categories. See the US Department of Labor's Web site at *www.dol.gov.*

25. See the Department of Labor's Web site at *http://www.dol.gov/whd/regs/compliance/childlabor102.pdf.*

United States and over half of those workers lack authorization to work legally in the United States.[26]

Cesar Chavez and the United Farm Workers

Cesar Chavez (1927–1993) is a widely recognized advocate and organizer in the US labor movement. Born in Arizona to a Mexican American family, Chavez spent most of his life in California, where he saw firsthand that many agricultural workers were being exploited for their labor. He started the United Farm Workers in 1962 to promote just working conditions and fair wages for people working in the agricultural sector of California. Chavez advocated for nonviolent means of change, including boycotts, fasting, and public witness. Many people look to him as a model for integrating Catholic spirituality and social thought into one's approach to justice.

Day laborers—individuals hired on an informal basis mainly for construction work, home repairs, moving assistance, and gardening—represent another especially vulnerable population in the US labor market. The majority of day laborers are employed in some form of construction work, which reports a high rate of job-related injuries. The Bureau of Labor Statistics listed the construction industry as having the highest number of work-related fatalities in 2009.[27] The immigration status of the majority of day laborers may increase their risk of injury in the construction industry. A recent study reported that the majority of these workers are Latino immigrants and 75 percent

---

26. US Department of Labor, National Agricultural Worker Survey, 2001–2002 Report Summary, available at *http://www.doleta.gov/agworker/report9/chapter1.cfm#summary*.

27. US Bureau of Labor Statistics, U.S. Department of Labor (2011) available online at *http://www.bls.gov/iif/oshwc/cfoi/cfch0008.pdf*.

are undocumented.[28] Without legal authorization to work, day laborers often take the most dangerous jobs and are afraid to oppose unsafe conditions.[29]

Social ethicist Kristin Heyer identifies a number of injustices day laborers experience. These include wage-theft[30] and exposure to unsafe working conditions.[31] Heyer draws on CST to advocate for the protection of workers' rights regardless of their legal status. Catholic teaching grounds human rights, including the rights of workers in human dignity, making them universal and intrinsic. Heyer applies this to the context of undocumented workers, arguing "undocumented workers and would-be workers are entitled to basic safeguards in light of longstanding Catholic social teachings on human rights and the rights of workers."[32]

Summary and Integration for Service Learners

The dignity of work is a central principle of CST. This chapter highlighted the development of this principle from *Rerum novarum* (*On the Condition of Labor*) to the personalist understanding of work in *Laborem exercens* (*On Human Work*). The personalist understanding of work articulated by Pope John Paul II emphasizes the central importance of the person as the subject of work and grounds the Church's critique of structures that lead to treating people as objects without rights and freedom. As a subject, the worker must be recognized as valuable and worthy of respect. Exploring work as a topic for social

---

28. Abel Valenzuela Jr., Nik Theodore, Edwin Melendez, and Ana Luz Gonzalez, "On the Corner: Day Labor in the United States" (January 2006), available at *http://www.sscnet.ucla.edu/issr/csup/index.php.*

29. Ibid.

30. Wage theft refers to a number of ways that employers unlawfully withhold wages from a worker. Some examples include failing to pay overtime, making an employee work off the clock, and failing to pay the legal minimum wage. See Kim Bobo, *Wage Theft in America: Why Millions of Working Americans Are Not Getting Paid—And What We Can Do About It*, second edition (New York: New Press, 2011).

31. Kristin Heyer, "Strangers in our Midst: Day Laborers and Just Immigration Reform," *Political Theology* Vol. 9, No. 4 (October 2008): 436.

32. Ibid., 426.

ethics invites reflection on how work enhances or diminishes the dignity of the worker.

With this foundation in mind, the USCCB has advocated for the dignity of work and the rights of workers. Drawing on CST, they have advocated for the right to work, the right to receive high enough wages to support oneself and one's family with dignity, and the right to working conditions that are worthy of the human person. US society today does not succeed in protecting these rights for all workers. Those employed in agriculture and as day laborers in construction are especially vulnerable to exploitation. Now that you have read about CST as it relates to work and information about the situation of some US workers, revisit your answers to the questions at the beginning of the chapter. Would you answer any questions differently? Use the following vignette and questions to practice aspects of the see-judge-act process in relation to this topic.

Unemployment

Service-Learning Vignette

A service learner working in an inner-city technology laboratory teaches computer skills to low-income adults. During her time in the technology lab, the student met a middle-aged man who had been unemployed for over a year after a back injury forced him to leave his job harvesting produce at a nearby farm. The student was amazed to discover that the man did not know how to use an Internet browser, making it impossible for him to search for jobs online. After talking with the man, the student learned that he had never owned a computer, and after dropping out of high school so he could work, he missed out on computer classes. Now, he feels behind on his ability to use technology and worries that it is going to hold him back from finding a job even though he has years of work experience. He told the student that he did not want to learn to use a computer but is willing to do whatever it takes to get back to work so he can support himself and his family.

See: Social Analysis

- What are some of factors that may be contributing to this man's long-term unemployment? Can you identify any possible injustices that may be factors?

- What are some possible background experiences that may have contributed to the student's access to technology and the man's lack of access? Can you identify any possible injustices that may account for the difference between the student's ability to use technology and the unemployed man's lack of ability?

Judge: Ethical Reflection

- Consider the situation of the man in the vignette in light of CST's principles of human dignity and the dignity of work. How might the principles of CST challenge the man's previous employers? How might the principles help to guide the work of those aiming to serve the unemployed?
- What is the difference between viewing workers as objects versus viewing them as subjects as articulated in CST? Does this understanding influence how you perceive the man in the vignette?

Act: Promoting Justice

- What might be done to address both the immediate and long-term needs of vulnerable workers and the unemployed? What specific policies and practices might support these efforts?
- Identify actions aligned with CST's call for the protection of the rights of workers that respond to the situation of vulnerable agriculture workers. Who is responsible for protecting the rights of such workers?

Suggestions for Further Social Analysis in a Service-Learning Context

- Research the unemployment rate in a particular area of a selected city, perhaps an area where a service-learning setting you are familiar with is located. Compare this rate with rates for other areas of the city, the state, and the country.
- Learn about the wage and labor laws in a selected city. Investigate whether some sectors of the workforce are vulnerable to violations of these laws.
- Learn more about a selected service organization that works to protect the rights of vulnerable workers. What problems

does it aim to solve, and what resources, programs, and services does it provide?

For Further Reading on Catholic Social Thought and Workers' Rights

Bobo, Kim. "Do Catholics Still Care about Labor?" *America* Vol. 193, Issue 5 (August 29, 2005): 10–13.

Finn, Daniel. "Human Work and Catholic Social Thought." *American Journal of Economics and Sociology* Vol. 71, Issue 4 (October 2012): 874–85.

Heyer, Kristin E. "Strangers in Our Midst: Day Laborers and Just Immigration Reform." *Political Theology* Vol. 9, Issue 4 (October 2008): 425–53.

O'Brien, John. *George G. Higgins and the Quest for Worker Justice: The Evolution of Catholic Social Thought in America.* Lanham, MD: Sheed & Ward, 2004.

Prouty, Marco G. *Cesar Chavez, the Catholic Bishops, and the Farmworkers' Struggle for Justice.* Tucson, AZ: University of Arizona Press, 2006.

CHAPTER 5

Economic Justice and the Preferential Option for the Poor

Introduction

The preferential option for the poor, which calls for putting the needs of people who are poor and vulnerable ahead of the needs of others, is a principle that can be traced back to the Hebrew Bible and the foundations of Christianity; however, it was not explicitly named in Catholic social teaching (CST) until recently. While the language of the preferential option for the poor does not appear in early social encyclicals, the principle is present implicitly whenever the teaching pays particular attention to the needs of the most vulnerable members of society. This attention reflects the central meaning of the preferential option for the poor—the people with the most need of charity and justice require the greatest response. Often described as the option for the poor and vulnerable, the application of this principle goes beyond the context of economic poverty to recognize other factors that can lead to marginalization, preventing people from full participation in society. Consider your understanding of poverty and the factors that lead people to impoverishment.

- What are some of the causes of poverty? What are some the ways impoverishment affects people?
- Identify some pathways a person might take to get out poverty. What obstacles might make following these pathways difficult? Who is responsible for alleviating poverty?
- Have you been involved in a service-learning setting that challenged or affirmed any of your ideas or assumptions about poverty?

This chapter will focus specifically on the issue of material poverty and examine the Catholic Church's teachings on economic justice. Consider your understanding of the economy and what economic justice means to you, using the following questions:

- What is the purpose of the economy? What signs indicate that a nation's economy is achieving its purpose?
- Who benefits the most and the least from the US economy as it is currently structured?
- What is economic justice? What values, principles, and priorities shape your understanding?

This chapter will trace the development of the principle of the preferential option for the poor in Catholic social tradition first by examining the influence of the bishops' conference of Latin America in conversation with the work of theologians and biblical scholars in articulating the preferential option for the poor. The theological reflection and action for justice that emerged in the context of Central and South America during the decades following Vatican II helped facilitate a shift in CST toward an explicit articulation of the preferential option for the poor.

This chapter will continue by discussing the United States Conference of Catholic Bishops' (USCCB) application of the principle of the preferential option for the poor in addressing poverty in the United States, giving particular attention to their 1986 pastoral letter, *Economic Justice for All*. The principles laid out in *Economic Justice for All*, particularly the preferential option for the poor, are made visible in the USCCB official initiative to address poverty in the United States, the Catholic Campaign for Human Development. Next the chapter will draw on social science data and the work of a contemporary theologian to help service learners better analyze and address poverty in the United States. The final section of the chapter provides a summary followed by a vignette drawn from an actual service-learning setting and a series of questions designed to help readers become more familiar with the see-judge-act process.

Preferential Option for the Poor in Catholic Social Teaching

The Call to Protect the Poor

Before the preferential option for the poor was specifically articulated as a major principle of CST, the early social encyclicals recognized the need to protect and care for the most vulnerable members of society. For example, in writings on the state's role in protecting workers, Popes Pius XI and Leo XIII expressed particular concern for the welfare of women and children, who they regarded as weaker members of society.[1] Also, for example, Pius XI expressed this concern in his 1931 encyclical *Quadragesimo anno* (*The Reconstruction of Social Order*): "The function of the rulers of the State, moreover, is to watch over the community and its parts; but in protecting private individuals in their rights, chief consideration ought to be given to the weak and the poor" (no. 25).

Early CST did not aim for radical social transformation. In *Rerum novarum* (*On the Condition of Labor*, 1891), Leo XIII, who believed that natural inequalities exist in society (no. 34), opposed the socialist agenda of leveling class distinctions. This view had implications for the Catholic Church's teaching on social justice. The early social encyclicals emphasized cooperation between social classes rather than the transformation of class structures in achieving justice for the poor. In *Rerum novarum*, Leo XIII argued that the Church could foster mutual love and goodwill among social classes necessary for eliminating the strife between the wealthy and the working class. He argues, "First of all, there is no intermediary more powerful than religion (whereof the Church is the interpreter and guardian) in drawing the rich and the working class together, by reminding each of its duties to the other, and especially of the obligations of justice" (no. 19).

---

1. Some today criticize early Catholic social teaching for being paternalistic, particularly with respect to women. It is important to locate the early social encyclicals in their historical contexts. Pope Leo XIII, like many people in that time period, believed that women were naturally suited for work in the home, and he wanted to protect this role. Feminist thinkers have pointed out the limitations of this view of women.

Later CST recognized that cooperation in unjust situations is difficult and emphasized the role of social transformation in promoting justice. Pope Paul VI, reflecting a global perspective and an awareness of the effects of colonization on the developing world, pointed out in *Populorum progressio* (*The Development of Peoples*, 1967), how structural inequalities perpetuate social conflict. With particular attention to the context of Latin America, the pope identified the connection between the suffering caused by extreme economic injustices and revolutionary uprisings:[2]

> The injustice of certain situations cries out for God's attention. Lacking the bare necessities of life, whole nations are under the thumb of others; they cannot act on their own initiative; they cannot exercise personal responsibility; they cannot work toward a higher degree of cultural refinement or a greater participation in social and public life. They are sorely tempted to redress these insults to their human nature by violent means. (No. 30)

Although the pope recognizes in *Populorum progressio* (*PP*) the temptation to resort to violent uprisings, he cautions against it, recognizing that such actions "engender new injustices, introduce new inequities and bring new disasters" (no. 31). Nevertheless, the pope argues for "profound changes" (no. 32) to correct the disparity of wealth perpetuating social conflict in developing countries.

In 1971 Paul VI called a synod (an international gathering of bishops) to address justice in the world. This synod, made up largely of bishops from Latin America, articulated in *Justice in the World* (*JW*) an explicit relationship between the Church's social mission and the transformation of unjust structures. The bishops affirmed that

---

2. El Salvador provides an example of the context to which Pope Paul VI was likely addressing. During the 1970s and 1980s a military-led government backed by the interests of a few wealthy landowners with US military aid violently resisted movements for reform of the country's oppressive economic inequalities. The conflict between the military government and the revolutionary guerrilla groups fueled a long civil war (1979–1992) in which thousands of people were killed or disappeared. For more information on the context, see Anna Lisa Peterson, *Martyrdom and the Politics of Religion: Progressive Catholicism in El Salvador's Civil War* (New York: State University of New York Press, 1997).

"Action on behalf of justice and participation in the transformation of the world fully appear to us as a constitutive dimension of the preaching of the Gospel" (no. 6). By emphasizing the social implications of the gospel message, the bishops direct the Church toward advocacy for the poor and oppressed. They ground their understanding of justice in a biblical view of God as a liberator of the oppressed: "In the Old Testament God reveals himself to us as the liberator of the oppressed and the defender of the poor, demanding from people faith in him and justice towards one's neighbor" (no. 30).

This section traced an important shift in CST that lays a foundation for the Catholic Church's contemporary understanding of the preferential option for the poor. The early social encyclicals of Leo XIII and Pius XI positioned the Church as a mediator between the rich and the poor, emphasizing the need for harmony and mutual respect between social classes. Following the writings of Paul VI, the 1971 synod of bishops observed that poverty oppressed people by limiting their ability to develop and flourish. Following this observation, the Catholic Church has positioned itself as an advocate for the poor and vulnerable.

The Contribution of Liberation Theology

A theological shift in the middle of the twentieth century shaped the Catholic Church's contemporary understanding of the preferential option for the poor. The shift involved the growing realization that theology is contextual, reflecting the historical and cultural realities out of which it emerges. The Second Vatican Council (1962–1965), which drew attention to both the importance of history and the Catholic Church's global nature, opened the doors for the emergence of new theologies that consider people's situation in life. This shift provided the context for the development of liberation theology, which aims to see reality from the perspective of the poor and the vulnerable and lifts up the preferential option for the poor as a key insight into what it means to be Christian.

When liberation theologians refer to poverty, they are not writing about a state of holiness that many have tried to achieve by embracing a life of simplicity. Rather, liberation theologians refer to poverty as an immediate reality that causes great suffering and may even impel faithful Christians to wonder if God is punishing them. When liberation theology emerged out of Latin America during the 1970s and 1980s, poverty was a leading cause of death in many communities. Out of this context, liberation theologians name poverty as a reality that diminishes human dignity and opposes life. One of the early voices in liberation theology was Peruvian priest Gustavo Gutierrez. He speaks to this perspective:

> Life, a gift from God, is also the first human right. The poverty and insignificance in which many people live violates that right. In effect, poverty means death, both physical death that is early and unjust, due to lack of the most basic necessities for life, and cultural death, as expressed in oppression and discrimination for reasons of race, culture or gender.[3]

Liberation theologians view poverty as a negation of life and therefore speak of it as a sin, specifically as a social sin because it is perpetuated by social structures and institutions (i.e., economic markets, trade agreements, tax policies, etc.). Redemption from social sin requires a transformation of the unjust structures that perpetuate the harm. This realization provides the basis for framing the Christian theme of salvation as liberation. Liberation theologians invite Christians to consider how God's redemptive action occurs not only in a personal relationship with Christ or in God's final judgment at the end of time but also in the midst of human history through the building of the kingdom of God. This realization provides a focus for the mission of the Catholic Church.

A meeting of the bishops' conference of Latin America (Consejo Episcopal Latinoamericano or CELAM) in 1968 at Medellin, Colombia, was important in the history of the Catholic Church and for CST. At Medellin, the bishops identified justice for the poor as a biblical mandate and made working for justice on behalf of the poor a

---

3. Gustavo Gutierrez, "Memory and Prophecy" in *Option for the Poor in Christian Theology*, ed. Daniel Groody (Notre Dame, IN: University of Notre Dame Press, 2007), 27.

El Salvador Martyrs

Liberation theology emerged not only through ideas but also through concrete actions for justice. Sometimes such actions threaten people who benefit from unjust structures. In the context of the Salvadoran civil war (1979–1992) and the conflict that preceded it, Church leaders became targets of military violence because of their advocacy for the poor. Many people consider these individuals to be martyrs (people who die as a result of their commitment to their faith). Archbishop Oscar Romero, who spoke against the repressive military government, was assassinated by a Salvadoran soldier in 1980. In 1989, six Jesuits along with their housekeeper and her daughter were assassinated in their home by a US-trained Salvadoran soldier. The murders of the six Salvadoran Jesuits in particular prompted many US citizens to examine their country's involvement in supporting and training the Salvadoran military. The Ignatian Solidarity Network developed in response to this issue and continues to commemorate the deaths of the Salvadoran martyrs as they advocate for social justice.[4]

priority. Echoing liberation theologians, the bishops associated poverty with structural injustices that perpetuate a cycle of marginalization and state-sponsored violence against people who called for reform. They use the language of liberation to describe God's action in history:

> The Latin American Church has a message for all men on this continent who 'hunger and thirst after justice.' The very God who creates men in his image and likeness, creates the 'earth and all that is in it for the use of all men and all nations, in such a way that created goods can reach all in a more just manner,' and gives them power to transform and perfect the world in solidarity. It is the same God who, in

---

4. See *http://ignatiansolidarity.net/*.

the fullness of time, sends his Son in the flesh, so that He might come to liberate all men from the slavery to which sin has subjected them: hunger, misery, oppression and ignorance, in a word, that injustice and hatred which have their origin in human selfishness.[5]

The observation that social and economic structures oppress people living in poverty provides the rationale for the preferential option for the poor. Some people find the language of the preferential option for the poor to be confusing or misleading. To say that God prefers some people over others seems to imply that God's love is subject to the same limitations as human love, suggesting that God's love is partial and prejudiced. Liberation theologians do not use this language to undermine the belief that God's love is universal, maximal, and nondiscriminatory. Rather, they argue that God offers a preferential concern for the poor because social structures disadvantage them. Biblical scholar Elsa Tamez explains this as follows:

> We say that the option of God for the poor is preferential in the sense that God loves all of God's creatures but has a preferential or special love for the poor precisely because of their disadvantaged position in an unequal and discriminating society. . . . The foundation of the option for the poor is the intention to end structural sin that produces dehumanization of the poor as well as those responsible for their poverty. In other words, we can affirm that precisely because the love of God is universal, God opts for the poor so that there may no longer be excluded persons in society.[6]

Liberation theology draws on the biblical understanding of the preferential option for the poor and places it at the center of the church's social mission.

---

5. CELAM, Documents from Medellin, in *Renewing the Earth: Catholic Documents on Peace, Justice and Liberation*, eds. David O'Brien and Thomas Shannon (New York: Doubleday, 1977), 3.

6. Elsa Tamez, "Poverty, the Poor and the Option for the Poor," in *Option for the Poor*, ed. Groody, 46.

The Reception of Liberation Theology

Liberation theology developed through the work of professional theologians such as Gustavo Gutierrez, the Latin American bishops, and laywomen and laymen who reflected on the meaning of the experiences of those who were poor in light of the gospel. The theology that emerged has not always been fully received by official leaders of the Catholic Church. In 1984, during the papacy of John Paul II, when Joseph Ratzinger (who became Pope Benedict XVI) was prefect for the Congregation for the Doctrine of the Faith, the Vatican issued a statement, "Instruction on Certain Aspects of the 'Theology of Liberation'." The document criticized some theologies of liberation for incorporating Marxist themes "not compatible with the Christian conception of humanity and society" (section VII, no. 8).[7] The instruction does, however, embrace the principle of the option for the poor, which became a more pronounced theme of CST after the development of liberation theology. This principle is now widely regarded as integral to the Christian message. Benedict XVI reflected this in a 2007 statement: "the preferential option for the poor is implicit in the Christological faith in the God who became poor for us, so as to enrich us with his poverty (cf. 2 Cor 8:9)."[8]

The United States Conference of Catholic Bishops on the Economy

The USCCB applied CST, including the principle of the preferential option for the poor, to economic life in their 1986 pastoral letter,

---

7. Congregation for the Doctrine of the Faith, "Instruction on Certain Aspects of the 'Theology of Liberation'" (Libreria Editrice Vaticana, 1984).

8. Pope Benedict XVI, Address of His Holiness Benedict XVI to the Bishops of Latin America and the Caribbean, Shrine of Aparecida, May 13, 2007, no. 3, available online at *http://www.vatican.va/holy_father/benedict_xvi/speeches/2007/may/documents/hf_ben-xvi_spe_20070513_conference-aparecida_en.html.*

Economic Justice for All. This section will examine the major themes of the text and highlight how these themes inform the bishops' anti-poverty initiative, the Catholic Campaign for Human Development.

The Context of *Economic Justice for All*

When the bishops formed a committee to draft a pastoral letter on economic justice in 1980, they intended to focus on a critique of Marxism. Archbishop Rembert Weakland, the chair of the committee, pushed the members to focus on the moral dimensions of capitalism instead, noting that this would be more relevant and challenging to the US context.[9] The committee's work coincided with the presidency of Ronald Reagan (1981–1989), whose approach to economics relied on tax cuts intended to increase consumer spending. Reagan, and others, advocated for little government interference in order to promote freedom in the market. Many Americans believe that this *laissez-faire* ("let it be") approach to capitalism results in a strong economy that ultimately benefits the whole society, while others critique unregulated free-market capitalism for prioritizing profit over the common good and leaving the impoverished behind without a safety net.

Since *Rerum novarum* (*On the Condition of Labor*), CST has offered a sustained critique of both liberal capitalism and socialism. The USCCB follows this tradition by neither endorsing nor fundamentally rejecting particular economic systems, nor do they attempt to create a new economy based on the principles of Catholic teaching. Rather, they draw on the themes of Catholic social thought, particularly human dignity, the call to community and participation, solidarity, and the preferential option for the poor to develop a framework for economic justice.

Though the USCCB did not endorse or reject particular economic systems in the document, they did offer critiques and concrete suggestions for how to improve the capitalist system of the United States. In doing so, the bishops recognized that they were taking

---

9. Charles Curran, "Reception of Economic Teaching in the United States," in *Modern Catholic Social Teaching: Commentaries and Interpretations,* ed. Kenneth Himes et al. (Washington, DC: Georgetown University Press, 2005), 478.

a stance on a controversial matter, and they anticipated that there would be debates among Catholics on the moral authority of their recommendations. The bishops identify their statements as *prudential judgments*, a term used in Catholic moral theology to distinguish reasonable suggestions on moral life from authoritative declarations about what is morally good or evil. In *Economic Justice for All* (*EJA*) they state,

> We know that some of our specific recommendations are controversial. As bishops, we do not claim to make these prudential judgments with the same kind of authority that marks our declarations of principle. But we feel obliged to teach by example how Christians can undertake concrete analysis and make specific judgments on economic issues. The church's teachings cannot be left at the level of appealing generalities. (No. 20)

The bishops are careful to distinguish prudential judgments from authoritative moral principles for a couple of reasons. First, they recognize that Catholics of good conscience can disagree on how to apply the principles of CST in actual contexts. The bishops claim to avoid dictating how Catholics should vote, recognizing the legitimate separation of church and state. Second, they identify themselves as religious leaders, as experts on Catholic faith and morality, not as economists, sociologists, or political scientists. Speaking to this, the USCCB states the following:

> In our letter, we write as pastors, not public officials. We speak as moral teachers, not economic technicians. We seek not to make some political or ideological point but to lift up the human and ethical dimensions of economic life, aspects too often neglected in public discussion. We bring to this task a dual heritage of Catholic social teaching and traditional American values. (*EJA*, no. 7)

Like the US bishops' 1983 pastoral letter on peace, *Economic Justice for All* was the result of a broad consultative effort that sought to integrate multiple perspectives. The bishops relied on the expertise of many others, including economists, workers, business owners, ministers, activists, and theologians. They describe the process of drafting the letter as involving "careful inquiry, wide consultation, and prayerful discernment" (*EJA*, no. 3), noting that they were enriched by the listening process. The result of this effort was nearly one-hundred pages of analysis of the economic context of the United States, with theological, biblical, and ethical reflection on that context. The bishops also made constructive suggestions for developing a more just US economy, describing their proposal as "a New American Experiment." The bishops' new American experiment was framed as a full realization of democracy, one that allowed everyone to participate in the American dream (*EJA*, nos. 295–297).

Themes of *Economic Justice for All*

The theme of participation is central to the bishops' vision of economic justice, and it provides a focus for organizing the major principles of the letter, including the principle of the preferential option for the poor. The bishops state boldly, "We judge any economic system by what it does *for* and *to* people and by how it permits all to *participate* in it" (*EJA*, no. 13). There are many ways a society can evaluate its economy. It can evaluate an economy based on how it promotes profit, production, or distribution. By naming participation as the criterion for judging an economy, the bishops are offering a personalist perspective on economic life, summed up in the statement, "The economy should serve people, not the other way around" (*EJA*, no. 13). Implicit in their statement are the following assumptions, which they directly state: that the economy has moral dimensions because it is a human activity and that the human dimension cannot be considered alongside other dimensions of the economy. A personalist approach to the economy argues that the human dimension must be the center of all economic life.

The bishops' focus on participation has a firm grounding in the Catholic social tradition, particularly in light of the principle of the call to community. The bishops emphasize participation within the community because of the theological assumption that God created human beings for relationship, making persons inherently social. Following the assumption that people are social beings, to exclude an individual from the life of community can be considered a violation of human potential. There are many ways an individual can be prevented from participating in the economic life of a community. The bishops describe patterns of economic exclusion:

> Within the United States, individuals, families, and local communities fall victim to a downward cycle of poverty generated by economic forces they are powerless to influence. The poor, the disabled, and the unemployed too often are simply left behind. . . . These patterns of exclusion are created by free human beings. In this sense they can be called forms of social sin. (*EJA*, no. 77)

By describing marginalization from the community as a form of social sin, the bishops link the Church's social mission with the work to overcome economic injustices. Again, social sin refers to the structures of injustice that perpetuate racism, sexism, and poverty. Redemption from social sin requires a transformation of unjust structures. In this case, the bishops are inviting people to participate in overcoming the social sins engendered in the cycle of poverty.

The right to participate in community is grounded in the principle of the common good as developed in CST. The bishops' insistence that everyone has the right and responsibility to participate in the common good provides a basic argument for the preferential option for the poor. When individuals are empowered to participate in social life, they strengthen the whole community. Recall that the Catholic social tradition refers to the common good to point to all that is produced in social life that allows the whole community to flourish. Although people rightly pursue a good life as individuals, CST calls people to pursue the common good. According to CST, the common good is not measured by the greatest good for the majority but rather by the flourishing of everyone. The commitment to the common good, therefore, involves a preferential commitment to the flourishing of the poor and vulnerable of a community.

The bishops offer a biblical and theological mandate for the preferential option for the poor in *Economic Justice for All*:

> Though in the Gospels and in the New Testament as a whole the offer of salvation is extended to all peoples, Jesus takes

the side of those most in need, physically and spiritually. The example of Jesus poses a number of challenges to the contemporary church. It imposes a prophetic mandate to speak for those who have no one to speak for them, to be a defender of the defenseless, who in biblical terms are the poor. It also demands a compassionate vision that enables the Church to see things from the side of the poor and powerless and to assess lifestyle, policies, and social institutions in terms of their impact on the poor. It summons the Church also to be an instrument in assisting people to experience the liberating power of God in their own lives so that they may respond to the Gospel in freedom and in dignity. (No. 52)

Drawing on Scripture, the bishops provide four points that summarize the grounds for and meaning of the preferential option for the poor in Catholic social thought. First, Jesus provides the mandate for the preferential option for the poor through his own example. Second, the biblical notion of poverty is connected to the state of powerlessness and marginalization. Third, the poor and vulnerable provide a vantage point from which to evaluate social structures and policies. Fourth, the Church's social mission involves being an instrument of God's liberating love for the vulnerable.

Catholic Campaign for Human Development

The USCCB's commitment to alleviating poverty predates their articulation of their economic justice in 1986 in *Economic Justice for All*. One of the most successful of the bishops' efforts is the Catholic Campaign for Human Development (CCHD), the largest privately funded self-help program for people living in poverty in the United States. The CCHD has distributed more than four hundred million dollars to various groups since its establishment in 1970. Unlike other Catholic-sponsored charitable organizations that offer direct assistance to those living in poverty, the CCHD's emphasis on social justice looks for long-term solutions that address the roots of poverty. The CCHD has developed into a unique program that directs its efforts to the empowerment of impoverished communities through self-led projects aimed at social change. Specifically, it funds community organizing efforts, new businesses in impoverished communities, and nonprofit programs that are led by the people most affected by the service. The USCCB manifests the principle of participation in the way they direct CCHD funds:

> For the purposes of CCHD funding, the participation of poor people in the shaping and ongoing direction of organizations is a central criterion. While "advisory" groups may also strengthen an organization, poor and low income people must have and maintain a strong voice in the organization's leadership both in terms of its governance structure and policy decisions, specially through their direct participation in the board of directors.[10]

Although the CCHD funds programs run by organizations that are not Catholic, it requires recipients to agree to promote the principles of Catholic social thought. In addition, the bishops see the CCHD as a vehicle to promote subsidiarity: "[The] CCHD focuses on local communities seeking to give voice to those closest to problems of poverty, as these communities address economic injustice working with local, state or national institutions to address the causes of poverty."[11] The rationale behind subsidiarity is that the people who are the most affected by social issues are the ones who have the best understanding of what they need. Following this rationale, social change should be led by the individuals most immediately affected by that change. Guided by the principle of subsidiarity and the preferential option for the poor, this approach to poverty promotes participation among communities that have been marginalized.

---

10. CCHD Basic Principles of Catholic Mission, available online at *http://www. usccb.org/about/catholic-campaign-for-human-development/grants/cchd-basic-principles-of-catholic-mission.cfm*.

11. CCHD, "Catholic Identity," available online at *http://www.usccb.org/about/catholic-campaign-for-human-development/frequently-asked-questions.cfm*.

The Catholic Worker Movement

The Catholic Worker movement is one of the most well-known, lay-led Catholic initiatives to serve and advocate for people living in poverty. Activist and journalist, Dorothy Day started the Catholic Worker with her friend, Peter Maurin in 1933 as a way to provide hospitality and basic necessities to people living in poverty. Day and other Catholic Workers embraced radical simplicity to live in community with the poor. *The Catholic Worker* was also the name of the newspaper they founded to promote nonviolence and social justice from a Catholic perspective. Today, the Catholic Worker movement includes many small communities across the United States that, inspired by the gospel and the example of Dorothy Day, choose to live and serve alongside people living in poverty.

Reading the Signs of the Times: Poverty and Empowerment

This section will further explore poverty and the economic life in the United States, focusing particularly on wealth inequality. It will provide information about the widening gap between the wealthy and the impoverished that can contribute to contemporary social analysis and explore theologian James Bailey's use of Catholic social thought to advocate for empowering the poor through asset building.

The 2010 US census reported a poverty rate of 15.1 percent of the US population, the highest rate of poverty recorded in fifty-two years of government measuring. This means that over forty-six million Americans (one in seven of the population) were living in poverty in 2010.[12] These numbers reveal only a part of the problem. Some economists argue that the way the official poverty threshold is

---

12. US Census Bureau 2010 Poverty Report available online at *http://www.census.gov/newsroom/releases/archives/income_wealth/cb11-157.html*.

measured in the United States is inadequate. Since the mid-1960s, the US government has employed the same method for measuring poverty, making slight adjustments for price changes. The poverty threshold is established by estimating the cost of food on a low-income budget. Assuming that a family spends one third of its income on food, the poverty threshold is three times the estimated food budget for a family, with the size of family taken into consideration. One of the limitations of this method is that it fails to take into account the economic changes that have occurred in the past fifty years. Today, economists point out, a typical US family spends more money on housing, transportation, and child care than fifty years ago when the poverty measure was developed. Therefore, it is inaccurate to assume that a family can still budget one-third of its income on food.[13] In fact, people living below or near the poverty line are forced to make difficult decisions between paying for basic necessities and making long-term investments in education, home-ownership, and retirement.

Although millions in the United States live near or below the poverty line, the United States is home to some of the wealthiest people in the world. Economists have noted the growing wealth disparity between the richest people in the United States and the majority of the population. The Economic Policy Institute measured wealth gain for the top 1 percent of the United States and found that this group secured 59.9 percent of the wealth gain (wages and capital income) between 1979 and 2007. An even smaller group, those representing the top 0.1 percent of the population secured 36 percent of wealth gain in the same period. This trend has concentrated the majority of wealth in the hands of a relatively small number of people. In 2009, the wealthiest 1 percent of the US population held 225 times the wealth of the median US household.[14]

---

13. Jared Bernstein, "Economic Opportunity and Poverty in America," (February 26, 2007) Economic Policy Institute, available online at *http://www.epi.org/publication/webfeatures_viewpoints_econ_oppty_and_poverty/*.

14. Lawrence Mishel and Josh Bivens, "Occupy Wall Streeters Are Right about Skewed Economic Rewards in the United States," (October 26, 2011) Economic Policy Institute, available online at *http://www.epi.org/publication/bp331-occupy-wall-street/*.

The shrinking middle class and growing wealth gap in the United States poses a number of ethical concerns. First, many people are unable to own their own homes and make long-term investments. Without the opportunity to build assets (homeownership, retirement, etc.), low-income people have limited opportunities to rise out of poverty. The US government provides a number of asset-building incentives—tax deductions or exemptions for mortgage interest, financial investments, and 401k retirement savings. However, many of these incentives exclude people who are unemployed, underemployed, or whose income does not allow them to make long-term investments. Theologian James Bailey points out the injustice of this situation, arguing the following:

> The United States already has in place a variety of initiatives that, taken together, constitute a vigorous and broad-based asset-building policy. The problem is that the beneficiaries of these policies are almost exclusively the nonpoor. Indeed, the current asset-based initiatives are so focused on the nonpoor that it would be accurate to characterize them as a "preferential option for the nonpoor."[15]

Bailey does not argue for an end to such asset-building programs, but rather stresses the need for broader participation among lower-income people. He sees asset building as an essential way to empower people to escape the cycle of poverty.

Bailey draws on Catholic social thought to emphasize the importance of asset building to alleviate poverty. Specifically, he argues that the themes of the common good, participation, and the preferential option for the poor all encourage broadened ownership and wealth distribution. Catholic social thought, he argues, also provides a framework for economic life that challenges the individualism that fuels the wealth gap in the United States. Referring to the common good, Bailey writes, "To the degree that ownership is correlated with greater participation at all levels of society, expanding the number of owners not only contributes to the individual good of these

---

15. James Bailey, *Rethinking Poverty: Income, Assets, and the Catholic Social Justice Tradition* (Notre Dame, IN.: University of Notre Dame Press, 2010), 18.

new owners but also to the good of all members of society."[16] This understanding of ownership fits well with the USCCB's emphasis on participation as a central characteristic of a just economy. It also speaks to the importance of the preferential option for the poor because within the framework of the common good, empowering the economically marginalized contributes to the flourishing of all.

Summary and Integration for Service Learners

This chapter traced the development of the preferential option for the poor in the Catholic social tradition. Rooted in Scripture, this theme became prominent in Catholic social thought through the influence of Latin American liberation theology. Today, the preferential option for the poor provides a basis for contemporary CST on economic justice. This is especially evident in the way that the USCCB has addressed poverty and economic life in the United States. This chapter also explored the USCCB's response to poverty through CCHD and their concern about the inequalities between the wealthy and impoverished in the United States today. Now that you have learned about CST as it relates to poverty and economic justice, revisit your responses to the questions at the beginning of this chapter. Would you answer any questions differently? Has the chapter challenged any of your ideas or assumptions about poverty and what should be done to address it? Use the following vignette and questions to practice aspects of the see-judge-act process in relation to this topic.

Navigating through Poverty

Service-Learning Vignette

A student serving meals at a residential program for families transitioning from homelessness met a woman who challenged some of his assumptions about poverty. The woman, a single mother of three, said that her family became homeless after she lost her job at a grocery store. She said she was fired after having to miss several days of work to care

---

16. Ibid., 49.

for her son who suffers from chronic ear infections. Making minimum wage, she could not afford to hire a babysitter to care for him and take him to the doctor. Living paycheck to paycheck, she said, did not allow her to save up for emergencies or periods of unemployment.

See: Social Analysis

- What are some social injustices that may be contributing to this woman's experience of homelessness? In addition to poverty, what other factors might contribute to her vulnerability?
- What obstacles might be preventing her from fully participating in the common good?

Judge: Ethical Reflection

- Using the criterion of participation as a measure of economic justice, how would you critique the social injustices you noted in answering the first question?
- How might the application of the preferential option for the poor have helped the woman in the vignette avoid homelessness? How might it be helping her now?

Act: Promoting Justice

- Based on what you have learned about CST's option for the poor and poverty in the United States today, what ideas might you have for alleviating poverty? What elements are essential for an antipoverty measure to work?
- How do you distinguish actions oriented toward charity and those oriented toward social justice? From your perspective, what is the role of each in implementing the principle of CST that calls for giving preference to the poor?

Suggestions for Further Social Analysis in a Service-Learning Context

- Using recent census data, research the median income for the neighborhood in which a service-learning setting you are familiar with is located. How does this income data compare with data for the United States in general and for the state and city in which the neighborhood is located?

- Identify some programs (private and public) aimed at assisting the poor or alleviating poverty. Establish criteria for assessing the success of these programs, and then evaluate them on that basis. What factors contribute to success?

- Compare the median income of people living in the neighborhood in which a service-learning setting you are familiar with is located with the estimated living expenses offered by the Consumer Expenditure Survey (*www.bls.gov/cex/*) for the same geographically area. What do you notice?

For Further Reading on Catholic Social Thought and Poverty

Bailey, James. *Rethinking Poverty: Income, Assets, and the Catholic Social Justice Tradition.* Notre Dame, IN: University of Notre Dame Press, 2010.

Bane, Mary Jo, and Lawrence Mead. *Lifting Up the Poor: A Dialogue on Religion, Poverty and Welfare Reform.* Washington, DC: Brookings Institution Press, 2003.

Groody, Daniel G. ed. *The Option for the Poor in Christian Theology.* Notre Dame, IN: University of Notre Dame Press, 2007.

Massaro, Thomas. *United States Welfare Policy: A Catholic Response.* Washington, DC: Georgetown University Press, 2007.

O' Neill, William. "Poverty in the United States." In *Resources for Social and Cultural Analysis: Reading the Signs of the Times,* Edited by T. Howland Sanks and John Coleman. New York: Paulist Press, 1993.

chapter 6

Promoting Solidarity in Peacemaking

Introduction

The concept of *solidarity* is used generally to describe people's interdependence with one another and their responsibility to act in ways that enhance their relationships with others. Solidarity challenges everyone to recognize all the ways that people are linked together and to strengthen the bonds that promote the good of all. Various leaders have at times used the value of solidarity as a rallying cry to encourage people to participate in works for the good of others, such as social movements, labor unions, the promotion of economic justice, and efforts to provide assistance across the globe. Reflect on your understanding of interdependence and solidarity and, if possible, connect these understandings to a service-learning setting.

- How do you define interdependence? Can you identify an example that illustrates the depth of the interdependence of people in your community? In what ways does the concept of *solidarity* cohere with or differ from your understanding of interdependence?

- Has your understanding of interdependence developed or changed in light of a service-learning experience you may have had? Have you encountered people acting in solidarity with others in a service-learning setting? Explain.

- Have you met people in a service-learning setting who have suffered injustice because they or others have ignored their interdependence with others? If so, what social issues seem to emerge from this? What information would you need to better identify, understand, and respond to these issues?

Catholic social teaching (CST) uses the principle of solidarity to articulate people's responsibility to respond to many injustices, including economic inequalities, abuse of the environment, unjust wars and violence, and human-rights violations. This chapter will focus on how the principle of solidarity has informed the United States Conference of Catholic Bishops' (USCCB) response to violence through the promotion of peace. As a global and local problem, violence breaks down communities, damages solidarity, and diminishes human dignity. Violence and its consequences affect communities in many ways. Consider how these may be affecting your community and people you may be familiar with through service learning.

- Has the community in which you live been affected by violence, such as abuse, exploitation, violent crime, or war? If so, has the community addressed this violence? Explain how.

- Have you met people in a service-learning setting who have been affected by violence? If so, has the community within which these people live addressed the violence? What information would you need to assess the affect violence may have on the people in this service-learning setting?

- What are some of the ways peace is maintained among the people you interact with most closely? How do these ways compare with those used by people in a service-learning setting with which you are familiar? Who takes responsibility for maintaining peace? What resources or skills do they use? What strategies promote peace effectively?

This chapter will examine how CST articulates the meaning and significance of solidarity and explore how this principle is applied by the USCCB in their response to violence. In their 1983 pastoral letter, *The Challenge of Peace: God's Promise and Our Response*, the USCCB addresses the moral dimensions of war, and drawing on the Catholic social tradition, they challenge people to promote peace. Ten years after *Challenge of Peace*, the USCCB issued another statement, *The*

Harvest of Justice Is Sown in Peace, which echoes many themes of the earlier pastoral letter but also reveals some significant developments. War, violence, and their consequences continue to pose ethical problems in the United States.

Next the chapter will examine some of the issues that US veterans face today, drawing on social science data and insights from Christian ethics. The final section of the chapter provides a summary followed by a vignette drawn from an actual service-learning setting and a series of questions designed to help readers practice aspects of the see-judge-act process.

The Principle of Solidarity in Catholic Social Teaching

Foundations of Solidarity in Early Teachings

The early social encyclicals do not rely on the word *solidarity*; however, the theme of human interdependence runs throughout the texts. Popes Leo XIII and Pius XI regard human interdependence as a reality and argue that society must reflect this unity through the peaceful cooperation of people from all social classes. The popes envisioned this cooperation being promoted with a spirit of benevolence through charitable practices. Pius XI argued that charity could not replace justice, understood as giving each person his or her due. However, charity, the pope argued, is indispensable because it promotes a sense of unity and commitment to the common good, which justice alone cannot achieve. Justice is important because it challenges people to recognize their obligation to the common good, but charity is essential because it promotes feelings of love and benevolence, which foster a sense of unity and kinship within society. Pius XI suggests in *Quadragesimo anno* (*The Reconstruction of Social Order*, 1931), "And so, then only will true cooperation be possible for a single common good when the constituent parts of society deeply feel themselves members of one great family and children of the same Heavenly Father" (no. 137).

International Solidarity as the Foundation for Peace

The early social encyclicals tended to focus on issues affecting the European Catholic Church. As CST became more international in scope, the concept of *solidarity* become more prominent in this teaching. Pope John XXIII was important in facilitating this shift. In 1961 he used the language of solidarity to address the responsibilities of wealthy, powerful nations toward impoverished ones. In *Mater et magistra* (*Christianity and Social Progress*, 1961), he states: "The solidarity which binds all men together as members of a common family makes it impossible for wealthy nations to look with indifference on the hunger, misery and poverty of other nations whose citizens are unable to enjoy even elementary human rights" (no. 157). John XXIII reflected on the connection between the promotion of human rights and peacebuilding in his encyclical *Pacem in terris* (*Peace on Earth*, 1963). According to the pope, human rights include cultural, political, and economic rights. He argues that nations should promote human rights in the spirit of solidarity, collaborating as much as possible for the common good of the entire human family (see *Pacem in terris*, no. 98). Reflecting his global perspective, John XXIII's encyclicals stress the importance of international solidarity in the pursuit of human development.

In *Populorum progressio* (*The Development of Peoples*, 1967), Pope Paul VI explicitly develops the connection between the promotion of human rights throughout the world and peacebuilding, exemplified in his often-quoted statement, "If you want peace, work for justice."[1] Recall that justice, from the perspective of Paul VI, could be achieved only through integral human development, development that extends beyond economic growth to the many dimensions of the human person. Promoting full human development, the pope insists in *Populorum progressio* (*PP*), is a responsibility of all nations and ultimately benefits every nation because it is the key to securing lasting peace:

---

1. Pope Paul VI, "World Day for Peace Message" (1972) available at *http://www. vatican.va/holy_father/paul_vi/messages/peace/documents/hf_p-vi_mes_19711208_ v-world-day-for-peace_en.html*.

When we fight poverty and oppose the unfair conditions of the present, we are not just promoting human well-being; we are also furthering man's spiritual and moral development, and hence we are benefiting the whole human race. For peace is not simply the absence of warfare, based on a precarious balance of power; it is fashioned by efforts directed day after day toward the establishment of the ordered universe willed by God, with a more perfect form of justice among men. (No. 76)

Paul VI connects the pursuit of peace with the alleviation of poverty and injustice—peace is not just the absence of war. Lasting peace can be achieved only by securing human rights and promoting integral human development. In CST, the principle of solidarity provides a rationale for international cooperation in this effort: by broadening one's responsibility for others beyond national, cultural, and ethnic boundaries, the work of promoting global justice becomes a responsibility of all.

Solidarity as a Christian Virtue

Pope John Paul II wrote on the topic of solidarity in *Sollicitudo rei socialis* (*On Social Concern*, 1987), his encyclical commemorating the twentieth anniversary of Paul VI's *Populorum progressio* (*The Development of Peoples*). In *Sollicitudo rei socialis* (*SRS*), John Paul II echoed many of his predecessor's insights on the connection between peace and international justice. John Paul II also retrieved insights from the early social encyclicals, emphasizing the role of charity in promoting a sense of unity necessary for the promotion of solidarity. The pope suggests that solidarity embraces the demands of justice but also goes beyond these demands by incorporating a spirit of generosity, which is rooted in his understanding of Christian discipleship:

In what has been said so far it has been possible to identify many points of contact between solidarity and charity, which is the distinguishing mark of Christ's disciples (cf. John 13:35). In the light of faith, solidarity seeks to go beyond itself, to take on the specifically Christian dimension of total gratuity, forgiveness and reconciliation. (*SRS*, no. 40)

John Paul II connects solidarity to Christian discipleship in two ways—providing a theological understanding of solidarity and describing solidarity as a virtue, an expression of moral life. He roots solidarity in the theological understanding that all people are part of a single family that exists in relationship with the one God, creator of all. The second Creation narrative in Genesis conveys this understanding by asserting that it is not good for a person to be alone (see Genesis 2:18). Christians interpret this to mean that human beings need relationships to thrive and develop. In light of this theological understanding, human interdependence is not accidental or a weakness to overcome. Rather, interdependence is rooted in God's intention that relationships have a central role in human existence.

John Paul develops this theological understanding further by pointing out that because people are created in the image and likeness of God the Trinity, they are called to reflect the loving communion that characterizes the relationships among the three persons of the Trinity:

> Beyond human and natural bonds, already so close and strong, there is discerned in the light of faith a new model of the unity of the human race, which must ultimately inspire our solidarity. This supreme model of unity, which is a reflection of the intimate life of God, one God in three Persons, is what we Christians mean by the word "communion." (*SRS*, no. 40)

This theological understanding of human relationships carries moral implications. Communion, as modeled in the life of the Trinity, provides a model for human relationships. These relationships are marked by love, mutuality, and commitment to the flourishing of the other. According to this model, people, being in God's image, should reflect these qualities in all aspects of their lives, which are inherently social.

The second way John Paul II connects solidarity to Christian discipleship is by presenting solidarity as a virtue. Virtues are habits and dispositions that orient people toward a moral good. Honesty, for example, is a virtue that orients a person toward a moral good, telling the truth. Solidarity is also a virtue because it involves habits and disposition that orient people toward taking responsibility for the common good. Taking responsibility for the common good involves recognizing not only that people are interdependent but also that the reality of interdependence has moral implications. John Paul suggests,

> When interdependence becomes recognized in this way [as a moral reality], the correlative response as a moral and social attitude, as a "virtue," is solidarity. This then is not a feeling of vague compassion or shallow distress at the misfortunes of so many people, both near and far. On the contrary, it is a firm and persevering determination to commit oneself to the common good; that is to say to the good of all and of each individual, because we are all really responsible for all. (*SRS*, no.38)

Articulating the theological meaning of solidarity and naming it as a Christian virtue, John Paul II provided important insights for CST that are relevant to the USCCB's approach to peacebuilding.

The United States Conference of Catholic Bishops on Peacebuilding

This section discusses the USCCB's articulation of norms and principles for peacebuilding and the virtues and character of a peacemaker and their contribution to the promotion of peace on multiple levels of society—not just in the face of war but also in people's everyday lives—in families, in the media, and so on.

The Context of the United States Conference of Catholic Bishops' *The Challenge of Peace*

The theme of solidarity runs throughout the USCCB's pastoral letter, *The Challenge of Peace: God's Promise and Our Response* (*CP*), in explicit and implicit ways as the bishops stress human interdependence as the moral foundation for peace. The letter presents two approaches to peace within the Christian tradition—just war and nonviolence—as well as the USCCB's judgments on specific peace-related issues, especially nuclear weapons and the global arms race.

The reality of modern warfare—with the potential to involve nuclear weapons and cause unprecedented amounts of destruction—created particular urgency for the bishops' message.

In addition to addressing specific issues related to modern warfare, the bishops spoke broadly about peace, articulating "a strong presumption against war" (CP, no. 70) and stressing that peace is more than the absence of war (CP, no. 68). Following the work of Pope John XXIII the USCCB states: "Peace is both a gift of God and a human work. It must be constructed on the basis of central human values: truth, justice, freedom and love" (CP, no. 68).

The USCCB connects the pursuit of peace to the identity of a Christian, claiming that this pursuit is a necessary part of following Christ. It states, "The Christian has no choice but to defend peace, properly understood, against aggression. This is an inalienable obligation. It is the *how* of defending peace which offers moral options" (CP, no. 73). The bishops consider both the just-war tradition and the tradition of nonviolence as morally acceptable approaches to achieving lasting peace and solidarity.

The Just-War Tradition and Pacifism

The just-war tradition offers guidelines for discerning when the use of force is morally legitimate, and it also offers principles for minimizing the harmful effects of war. The tradition of nonviolence or pacifism promotes peace with nonviolent means, opposing war and other forms of violence. Each of these traditions has a solid grounding in the Christian tradition and has developed historically as the Catholic Church has discerned how to live out the gospel mandate to seek the kingdom of God.

The traditions of just-war and pacifism may strike some readers as contradictory. Pacifists claim that it is morally wrong to oppose violence with violence, while those who advocate for the just-war tradition explain that violence is sometimes necessary in the defense of peace. The USCCB suggests that these approaches are not contradictory but are complementary ways to promote the ideal of peace in an imperfect world marked by violence. In its view, the Christian understanding of the kingdom of God in history grounds the Christian responsibility to build peace:

> Christians are called to live the tension between the vision of
> the reign of God and its concrete realization in history. The
> tension is often described in terms of "already but not-yet":
> i.e., we already live in the grace of the kingdom, but it is not
> yet the completed kingdom. . . . In the kingdom of God,
> peace and justice will be fully realized. Justice is always the
> foundation for peace. In history, efforts to pursue both peace
> and justice are at times in tension, and the struggle for justice
> may threaten certain forms of peace. (*CP*, nos. 58, 60)

In other words, the bishops recognize that Jesus' vision of the
kingdom of God was marked by peace, making it the Christian
ideal. At the same time, the kingdom of God is not fully present
in history. It is something that Christians long for, work for, and
pray for. In the messiness of human history, the world experiences
injustices, such as genocide, widespread violence against women,
and other atrocities. Recognizing this imperfect context, the question becomes, "How do Christians live into the kingdom of God in
a world marked by injustices?"

Advocates of the just war theory do not rule out the use of force
to address injustices. However, the just-war tradition presumes a
strong preference to avoid violence in the promotion of peace. The
just-war tradition emerged in the fifth century when Saint Augus-
tine asked under what conditions Christians could use violence to
defend Rome against invasion. Concluding that Christians could
not be obligated to pursue pacifism at all costs, he began to develop
guidelines for limiting the use of violence. The just-war tradition,
from the beginning, actively promoted peace.

The just-war tradition seeks to minimize the harmful effects of
war by outlining guidelines for discerning when it is just to go to war
(*jus ad bellum*) and what strategies are just during times of war (*jus
in bello*). The USCCB lists these principles in *Challenge of Peace* (see
no. 85 ff.). The criteria for going to war include having a just cause,
which does not include retribution. The bishops state that there must
be a "real and certain danger" to innocent human life or human rights
(*CP*, no. 86). A just war also must follow the right intention, namely,
the pursuit of peace against an imminent threat. A just war must also
meet the criteria of being declared by a competent authority that

wages war as a last resort after exhausting nonviolent alternatives. Finally, the moral acceptability of going to war is determined by the principles of comparative justice, proportionality, and the probability of success. In other words, the justice or good achieved by war must be worth the costs (*CP*, no. 99).

The main criteria for maintaining justice within war are proportionality and discrimination. The principle of proportionality requires tactics and strategies during war to be proportionate to the threat at hand. The principle of discrimination requires that the use of force be directed toward unjust aggressors, maintaining noncombatant immunity. The bishops note that the principles of proportionality and discrimination eliminate the legitimacy of total war, a war that would mean death for large numbers of innocent people (*CP*, no. 104). The bishops condemn such warfare, even to defend the innocent and most vulnerable. Specifically, they propose a preferential concern for the most vulnerable during times of war, stating, "It is of the utmost importance, in assessing harms and the justice of accepting them, to think about the poor and the helpless, for they are usually the ones who have the least to gain and the most to lose when war's violence touches their lives" (*CP*, no. 105).

Recognizing that all wars (just or unjust) threaten human life has led some people to adopt a pacifist approach to peacebuilding. The USCCB recognizes that God calls some Christians to manifest the ideal of the kingdom of God by adopting such an approach. Christian pacifists stress that peace is integral to Jesus' vision of the kingdom of God and that in his uncompromising dedication to the kingdom, Jesus demonstrated a commitment to nonviolence. In the Beatitudes, Jesus identifies peacemakers as the "children of God" (Matthew 5:9), naming nonviolence as a central commitment of Christian discipleship. Some Christian pacifists choose nonviolence because Jesus offered a nonviolent example in the face of a violent death on the cross.

The USCCB praises the moral fortitude of individuals who follow Jesus' example of nonviolence and commit themselves to Christian pacifism, as witnesses to the kingdom of God. They stress that Christian nonviolence is not passive but it "affirms and exemplifies what it means to resist injustice through non-violent methods" (*CP*, no. 116). The bishops credit the nonviolent witness of well-known pacifist Mahatma Gandhi, an Indian Hindu, as well as Dorothy Day

Promoting Justice after War, *Jus Post Bellum*

Christian ethicists continually evaluate the appropriateness and applicability of the just-war criteria. Stressing the importance of ongoing solidarity in the aftermath of war, some modern ethicists have suggested criteria for post-war justice or *jus post bellum*. Mark Allman and Tobias Winright propose the following criteria: just cause (leave the affected area in a more just and stable condition than prior to war), reconciliation (take responsibility for wrongdoing, reinforcing accountability and forgiveness), punishment (exact any punishments with transparency, proportionality, and a legitimate authority, often a third party), and restoration (address the economic, ecological, and social effects of the war).[2]

and Martin Luther King for having a profound impact on the church in the United States (*CP*, no. 117).

The bishops not only applaud individuals in history who have embraced nonviolence but they also defend the right of an individual to resist participation in military combat if conscience dictates. Thus, the bishops argue for legal protection of conscientious objectors, those who oppose military service on the basis of their moral and religious principles, as well as selective conscientious objectors, which refers to individuals who reject some but not all practices of military service (*CP*, no. 118). For example, a selective conscientious objector may be engaged in combat but refuse to use certain tactics that could endanger noncombatants, such as airstrikes. The bishops have continued to advocate for legal protection of conscientious objectors in the United States, where conscientious objection is granted as a privilege to individuals that meet strict conditions, but it is not considered to be a legal right.[3]

---

2. Mark J. Allman and Tobias L Winright, "When the Shooting Stops," *Christian Century* Vol. 127, Issue 20 (October 2010): 26–29.

3. Pax Christi USA, "Conscientious Objection and the Military" available at *http://paxchristiusa1.files.wordpress.com/2011/02/conscientious-objection-and-the-military-brochure.pdf.*

The USCCB refers to the Second Vatican Council to support the rights of conscientious objectors (*CP*, no. 118), quoting number 79 of *Gaudium et spes* (*Pastoral Constitution on the Church in the Modern World*, 1965), which explicitly addresses the rights of conscientious objectors, "Moreover, it seems right that laws make humane provisions for the case of those who for reasons of conscience refuse to bear arms." (*CP*, no. 118). This statement is significant because before the council, the Catholic Church did not support conscientious objection. Less than ten years before Vatican II, in 1956, Pope Pius XII declared that conscientious objection to a lawful war was not an option for individuals: "a Catholic citizen cannot invoke his own conscience in order to refuse to serve and fulfill those duties the law imposes."[4] The US bishops also rejected the legitimacy of conscientious objection throughout the first half of the twentieth century. Their position was consistent with the papal teaching of the time and was amplified by their interest in dispelling the widespread accusation that Roman Catholics were unpatriotic. Social ethicist Todd Whitmore describes how this influenced the bishops' public stance on conscientious objection, "Here, the issue of war arises not as a moral question about taking another person's life on behalf of the state but as a statement marking the boundaries, or the lack thereof, of American Catholic loyalty to the United States."[5] Today, US Catholics mirror the wider population in terms of their political commitments and expressions of patriotism.

The Harvest of Justice Is Sown in Peace

On the tenth anniversary of *The Challenge of Peace*, the USCCB revisited the relationship between pacifism and just war, publishing *The Harvest of Justice Is Sown in Peace* (*HJ*) in 1993. In it, the bishops reaffirm their support for pacifism and just-war as moral options for

---

4. Pope Pius XII, "Christmas Radio Message" (December 23, 1956) in Harry Flannery, ed. *Pattern for Peace: Catholic Statements on International Order* (Westminster MD: Newman Press, 1962), 283.

5. Todd Whitmore, "The Reception of Catholic Approaches to Peace and War in the United States," in *Modern Catholic Social Teaching: Commentaries and Interpretations*, ed. Kenneth Himes, et al. (Washington, DC: Georgetown University Press, 2005), 495.

the promotion of peace. Scholars note an important shift in the bishops' treatment of the role of collective acts of nonviolence. After the publication of *The Challenge of Peace* in 1983, the world witnessed nonviolent strategies that overcame and replaced totalitarian regimes in the Philippines and Eastern Europe. These movements illustrated the power of solidarity in overcoming injustice without the use of force. The bishops refer to these events saying,

> Although nonviolence has often been regarded as simply a personal option or vocation, recent history suggests that in some circumstances it can be an effective public undertaking as well. . . . One must ask, in light of recent history, whether nonviolence should be restricted to personal commitments or whether it also should have a place in the public order with the tradition of justified and limited war. (*HJ*, nos. 31, 33)

This marks a development from *The Challenge of Peace* when the bishops insisted that pacifism was an option for individuals and discussed it mainly within their defense of conscientious objection. In *The Harvest of Justice* the bishops took their commitment to nonviolence further, emphasizing nations' moral responsibility to explore the potential of effective nonviolence before resorting to violent conflict. The bishops also articulated this principle in *The Challenge of Peace*; however, between 1983 and 1993, the USCCB developed an enhanced appreciation for the proliferation of deadly weapons systems and the world witnessed nonviolent revolutions. These two developments led the bishops to become more skeptical about the use of force.

The bishops argue that the commitment to nonviolence must be fostered on both individual and collective levels. One of the ways that the bishops promote this is through reflecting on the spirituality of peacemaking. Spirituality, broadly speaking, refers to the way that an individual lives out his or her relationship with God. It touches on many aspects of one's faith life—prayer, religious devotions, and moral living. A spirituality of peacemaking allows people to develop practices that integrate the pursuit of peace into the way that they live out their faith. In *The Harvest of Justice*, the bishops connect Christian spirituality and peacemaking by encouraging all Christians to develop the virtues and vision of a peacemaker as an aspect of their faith life. Some of the virtues the bishops relate to the pursuit of peace are faith, hope, courage, compassion, kindness, and perseverance (*HJ*, no. 18).

Pax Christi USA

Pax Christi USA, affiliated with the multinational Catholic Pax Christi International, promotes peacebuilding through education and advocacy. Pax Christi USA works closely with Catholic parishes and bishops as well as other Christians to address specific threats to peace, including war, nuclear weapons, and violence. The organization emphasizes the need to promote peace on multiple levels—among nations and different communities in the United States, within families, and within one's own heart. Following this emphasis, they offer resources to connect Christian spirituality and peacebuilding. For more information, see their Web site at *www.paxchristiusa.org.*

These virtues are rooted in and motivated by a particular vision of peace. The vision of peace, which emerges from the insights of CST on solidarity, can be achieved only through a commitment to the global common good. The USCCB summarizes this vision, drawing on the Catholic social tradition:

> [T]he Church's positive vision of a peaceful world includes: the primacy of the global common good for political life, the role of social and economic development in securing the conditions for a just and lasting peace, and the moral imperative of solidarity between affluent, industrial nations and poor, developing ones. (*HJ*, no. 21)

The principle of solidarity is central in this vision of peacemaking because it challenges unjust relationships that create the conditions of conflict. The bishops identify specific expressions of solidarity that strengthen the bonds of unity between nations. Solidarity involves promoting human rights across national, ethnic, religious, and cultural differences. Solidarity also demands international aid that supports human development and closes the extreme gap between wealthy and impoverished nations. The bishops advocate for institutions to promote these expressions of solidarity (*HJ*, no. 24). By emphasizing the importance of solidarity in peacebuilding, the bishops reinforce the connection between justice and peace.

Reading the Signs of the Times: Social Justice for US Veterans

War poses a number of ethical dilemmas, each of which demands careful analysis, reflection, and response. The most recent wars involving the United States, those in Iraq and Afghanistan, have caused thousands of military and civilian deaths. This section of the chapter will focus on the consequences of these wars for US veterans. This focus will provide a way to examine features of modern warfare and its consequences for military personnel. Drawing on the insights of US bishop and ethicist, Robert McElroy, this section will analyze some of the implications of modern warfare in light of CST with the Catholic social tradition.

After returning from Iraq and Afghanistan, many US soldiers face a number of hardships. These may include financial instability and mental and physical health problems. The Department of Veteran Affairs provides assistance with healthcare, education, insurance, home loans, and counseling services to veterans. However, many veterans do not access these services, reportedly for a variety of reasons. Of particular significance are reports that veterans encounter barriers to access the mental health services, including difficulty securing appointments and reluctance to seek treatment due to fear of stigma or embarrassment.[6]

---

6. George H. Avery and Shelley M. MacDermid Wadsworth, "Access to Mental Health Services for Active Duty and National Guard TRICARE Enrollees in Indiana" *Military Medicine* Vol. 176 Issue 3 (March 2011): 261–64.

Public health experts have noted high levels of combat stress and other mental disorders among veterans, many of whom have received insufficient treatment. A 2009 report indicated that 21.8 percent of the 289,328 veterans of the wars in Iraq and Afghanistan have been diagnosed with Post Traumatic Stress Disorder (PTSD) and 17.4 percent have been diagnosed with depression.[7] Some scholars predict an even higher level of PTSD among veterans of these wars compared to previous wars. Factors contributing to high rates of PTSD include the type of fighting the soldiers have engaged in and the kind of preparation soldiers received. Wars like that carried out in Iraq, characterized by "urban street-fighting, civilian combatants and terrorism," may lead to an increased risk of PTSD among veterans.[8] Furthermore, 40 percent of the soldiers who have served in Iraq are members of the National Guard with less military training than members of the regular forces, leaving them more vulnerable to PTSD.[9]

Mental health problems and combat-related disabilities make it difficult for many veterans to secure employment. With many Iraq and Afghanistan veterans returning home to an economic recession, they face a high national unemployment rate. In 2011, the jobless rate for Iraq and Afghanistan veterans was slightly higher than for the rest of the US population at 11.1 percent. However, it was much higher among young veterans between the ages of eighteen and twenty-four. This group faced an unemployment rate of 37.9 percent in 2011.[10] Despite national programs to help veterans find jobs, many veterans experience difficulties translating their military skills into a nonmilitary career. For young soldiers competing with peers that already have targeted work experience, it can be particularly difficult to find employment. This leads to financial instability among many young veterans. Financial instability is one of the contributing factors

---

7. K. H. Seal; T. J. Metzler, K. S. Gima, D. Bertenthal, S. Maguen, and C. R. Marmar, "Trends and Risk Factors for Mental Health Diagnoses among Iraq and Afghanistan Veterans Using Department of Veterans Affairs Health Care, 2002–2008" *American Journal of Public Health*, Vol. 99:9 (September 2009): 1651–58.

8. Peg Tyre, "Battling the Effects of War," *Newsweek* Vol. 144, Issue 23 (December 6, 2004).

9. Ibid.

10. "A Hard Homecoming" *Economist*, Vol. 401, Issue 8764 (December 17, 2011).

to the high rate of homelessness among US veterans. Today, veterans make up an estimated 41 percent of the homeless population.[11]

The emotional, physical, and economic hardships that many US veterans face can go unnoticed. Less than 1 percent of Americans have served in the Iraq and Afghanistan wars. One credible survey, for example, reported that 84 percent of Iraq and Afghanistan veterans think that the general US population fails to understand the struggles that military personnel and their families face.[12] The presence of a professional military and the elimination of the military draft allow many American voters and policy makers to remove themselves from the moral implications of warfare.

The year 2011 marked the eleventh year of war between the United States and Afghanistan, making it the longest declared war in US history to date. Social ethicist and Catholic bishop Robert McElroy analyzes some of the features of modern warfare that have allowed the war in Afghanistan to continue for so long. With a huge military budget, advances in military technology that reduce American casualties, and a professional military that eliminates the draft and narrows the population immediately affected by the loss and trauma of US soldiers, McElroy concludes that, unlike previous eras of American history, "the United States has now achieved the capacity to wage major warfare over many years without greatly burdening its economy or general citizenry."[13] This context has allowed the United States to pursue the wars in Iraq and Afghanistan, both of which, McElroy suggests, lack a clear and attainable goal. Driven by the indefinite pursuit of societal transformation and the promotion of democracy, these wars led McElroy to suggest in 2011 that "the United States suffers from a paralyzing inability to bring wars to a close."[14] McElroy considers the

11. Eric B. Elbogen, Sally C. Johnson, Ryan H. Wagner, Virginia M. Newton, and Jean C. Beckham, "Financial Well-Being and Postdeployment Adjustment among Iraq and Afghanistan War Veterans" *Military Medicine* Vol. 177 Issue 6 (June 2012): 669–75.

12. Pew Research Center, "War and Sacrifice in the Post 9/11 Era" (October 5, 2011) available online at *http://www.pewsocialtrends.org/2011/10/05/war-and-sacrifice-in-the-post-911-era/*.

13. Robert McElroy, "War without End," *America* (February 21, 2011): 11.

14. Ibid., 12.

war in Afghanistan to be "a moral hazard for the world and for the identity of the United States"[15] that continued without provoking widespread outrage because only a small percentage of US citizens who enter the military "absorb the terrible trauma of casualties in war."[16] In order to promote peace, McElroy argues all US citizens "must recognize that war inevitably brings horrendous unintended consequences."[17]

United States Conference of Catholic Bishops Respond to Wars in Iraq and Afghanistan

The USCCB has addressed the ethical dimensions of the wars in Iraq and Afghanistan throughout the multiple stages of these wars' development. Writing in 2011, they emphasized responsible transition that will bring US military troops out of Afghanistan and Iraq in a way that minimizes further damage to the societies; protects the most vulnerable; and builds solidarity among the US, Afghani, and Iraqi peoples. In a 2011 statement on the war in Afghanistan, the bishops invited the Obama administration to consider the probability of success in securing Afghanistan against al Qaeda given how terrorism functions on a global scale. They also invited the administration to "continually review the use of military force—whether and when force is needed to protect the innocent and resist terrorism—to insure that it is proportionate and discriminate."[18]

15. Ibid.
16. Ibid., 11.
17. Ibid., 13.
18. USCCB Office of International Justice and Peace, "Background on Afghanistan-Pakistan" (February 2011) available at *www.usccb.org*.

Summary and Integration for Service Learners

This chapter explored the ethical dimensions of war and the Catholic Church's ongoing struggle to promote peace in a world marked by violence. As articulated by the USCCB in *The Challenge of Peace*, Christians are called to be peacemakers, making it an important theme in Catholic social thought. The USCCB recognizes that for some, this involves an uncompromising commitment to nonviolence. Pacifists witness to the ideal of peace that the church believes is a characteristic of the kingdom of God. For individuals who believe the demands of justice sometimes require the use of force, the just-war theory provides ethical guidelines for ensuring that violent conflict is morally justified (*jus ad bellum*) and for minimizing the devastating effects of violence (*jus in bello*). The US bishops have recognized the legitimacy of pacifism and the just-war approach but have noted that, as the destructive potential of modern warfare increases, the need for nonviolent solutions has become more urgent.

The principle of solidarity, as developed in the Catholic social tradition, provides a rationale for promoting peace through reinforcing just relationships between individuals and nations. By emphasizing human interdependence, solidarity calls us to lay the foundation for peace through promoting integral human development. Solidarity should also be fostered as a virtue, a habitual disposition or character trait that animates one's moral life. Framed in this way, peacemaking is a job not only for politicians and diplomats. Rather, everyone has the responsibility to become a peacemaker in daily life, recognizing human interconnectedness and responding justly.

Consider again your understanding of solidarity and peacemaking by revisiting the questions at the beginning of the chapter. Would you change any of your responses? What does solidarity mean to you now? What have you learned about violence and peace that might help you understand your own community and other communities? What might help you to better see or analyze a particular situation? How can the Catholic social tradition help you make judgments about unjust situations and determine the actions that promote justice in a particular context, including service-learning settings? Use the following vignette to practice the see-judge-act process.

Meeting a Veteran

Service-Learning Vignette

As part of his service learning, one student participated in a recovery circle for people whose lives have been affected by substance abuse. During the hour, the student met a man in his mid-twenties who is currently homeless and struggling to overcome an addiction to alcohol. Listening to his story, the student discovered that the man was married with two young children and had a home but lost everything due to his drinking. The man said that he began drinking after his tour of duty in Afghanistan to cope with feelings of anxiety. He had been diagnosed with PTSD but did not seek treatment because he did not want the alcohol abuse to be on his military record. He said that he feels alone and does not understand how he ended up in this position.

See: Social Analysis

- What are some of the factors that may have contributed to this man's homelessness? How much of his situation can be attributed to his decisions and how much can be attributed to factors outside of his control—to other social, political, economic, or cultural realities?

- What are some of the possible reasons for this man's isolation? What has contributed to his experience of access to the Veterans Administration benefits available to him?

Judge: Ethical Reflection

- Reflect on the vignette in light of CST, and determine how you would apply the principle of solidarity to the homeless man's situation. Have breakdowns in solidarity likely contributed to his situation? Do you see possible evidence that people have related to the man in a manner that aligns with the Catholic Church's vision of solidarity? What might need to change to promote the vision of solidarity developed in CST?

- What information would you need to apply the principles of just war to the recent wars in Iraq and Afghanistan? Do any of the principles of just war address the reality of the veteran in the vignette?

Act: Promoting Justice

- Based on what you have learned about CST and some of the problems that current veterans face in the United States, what specific actions might be taken to promote justice for this population? What structures, interests, or beliefs might hinder these proposed actions?
- What specific actions could be taken (by individuals, nations, and the international community) to reinforce solidarity and enhance the possibilities for nonviolent conflict resolution?

Suggestions for Further Social Analysis in a Service-Learning Context

- Research different perspectives on how to define violence and then gather data on violence as it relates to a service-learning setting. What is the rate of violent crime in the community? How does it compare with surrounding neighborhoods? Has it gone up or down in recent history?
- Research theories on the affects of violence. Is a person's gender, age, religion, race, geographical location, or socioeconomic level a factor in the way violence affects her or him? Does violence affect some communities more than others? Explain. How do these theories contribute to the analysis of the situations of people in a service-learning setting with which you are familiar?
- Investigate how a selected neighborhood or city addresses violence. What is the relationship with the police? What community led initiatives or nonprofit organizations are available to address violence in the community?

For Further Reading on Catholic Social Thought and Peacebuilding

Allman, Mark and Tobias Winright. *After the Smoke Clears: The Just War Tradition and Post War Justice.* Maryknoll, NY: Orbis Press, 2010.

Appleby, Scott, Robert Schreiter, and Gerard Powers, eds. *Peacebuilding: Catholic Theology, Ethics, and Praxis.* Maryknoll, NY: Orbis Press, 2010.

Fahey, Joseph. *War and the Christian Conscience: Where Do You Stand?* Maryknoll, NY: Orbis Press, 2005.

Massaro, Thomas and Thomas Shannon. *Catholic Perspectives on Peace and War.* Lanham, MD: Rowman & Littlefield, 2003.

Whitmore, Todd. "The Reception of Catholic Approaches to Peace and War in the United States." In *Modern Catholic Social Teaching: Commentaries and Interpretations*, edited by Kenneth Himes, et.al. Washington, DC: Georgetown University Press, 2005.

Care for Creation and Environmental Issues

Introduction

As evidence of global climate change grows and the availability of nonrenewable resources diminishes, more people are reflecting on their relationship to the natural world and searching for ways to promote responsibility toward the environment. Religious voices have emerged alongside secular approaches to environmental ethics. Christianity offers many resources for developing environmental ethics, including the theological themes of stewardship, incarnation, and sacrament. Each of these theological themes has been important in developing an ethical response to the environment within the Catholic social tradition. Before learning about the Catholic Church's approach to environmental ethics, reflect on your understanding of humanity's relationship to the natural world.

- Is the proper treatment of the natural world a moral issue in your view? If so, when did it become so for you? Has your awareness of it developed over time? What are the beliefs, values, and priorities behind your position?

- What are some ways you or people in your community have been affected by the degradation of the environment? How does your community address environmental issues? What kinds of resources are available to people in your community who want to exercise responsibility toward the environment?

- Consider the effects of environmental degradation on the people in a service-learning setting with which you are familiar. How do these effects compare with those experienced by people in your community? How does the community in which the service-learning setting is located address the abuse of the environment? What kinds of resources are available to people in that community who want to exercise responsibility for the environment?

* Do tensions exist between meeting fundamental human needs and caring for the environment? If so, do you notice differences in the ways various communities you are familiar with resolve these tensions? If so, what might account for the differences?

This chapter will trace the development of Catholic social teaching's (CST) call for the care for creation and will highlight how this principle guides responses to environmental issues. The theme is largely absent in the social encyclicals until the work of Pope Paul VI. Recent popes, John Paul II and Benedict XVI, have made the care for creation a priority in modern CST, issuing a strong critique of consumerism and individualism in their environmental ethic. Responding to this development, the United States Conference of Catholic Bishops (USCCB) has applied the principle of the care for creation to concrete environmental problems including global climate change. This chapter will examine the teaching of the USCCB on the environment and conclude by drawing attention to the connection between racism and environmental degradation.

Before reading further, reflect on environmental problems and how consumerism and racism might influence them.

* Are consumerism and the condition of the environment related? What attitudes and institutions perpetuate consumerism? Who and what aspects of the natural world benefit from it? Who and what aspects of the natural world are harmed by it?

* Do you observe a connection between racial discrimination and environmental degradation in your community or other communities you are familiar with through service learning? If so, what information would you need to determine if racism is a causal factor in this environmental degradation?

* How might a person's socioeconomic status affect the extent to which he or she is affected by problems in the environment?

This chapter will delve into the concept of stewardship of the earth as developed within CST by examining Pope Paul VI's *Octogesima adveniens* (*A Call to Action*) from 1971 when the growing awareness of moral issues in regard to the environment were relatively new. It will then look at the synod of bishops' statement, *Justice in the World* also from 1971 that discusses the environment and its resources as part of globalization and the call for the recognition of the inter-related nature of humanity. John Paul II and Benedict XVI continue the discussion of the disproportionate impact of environmental destruction on impoverished and marginalized communities in John Paul II's 1990 World Day of Peace message *Peace with God the Creator, Peace with All of Creation* and Benedict XVI's 2009 social encyclical, *Caritas in veritate* (*Charity in Truth*).

The chapter will also examine some ways the USCCB has focused on the principle of care for creation and their application of the principle to specific ecological issues by exploring two letters: *Renewing the Earth: An Invitation to Reflection and Action on Environment in Light of Catholic Social Teaching* (1991) and *Global Climate Change: A Plea for Dialogue, Prudence and the Common Good* (2001). The final section of the chapter provides a summary followed by a vignette drawn from an actual service-learning setting and a series of questions designed to help readers practice aspects of the see-judge-act process.

Care for Creation in the Catholic Social Tradition

Early Catholic Social Teaching on the Environment

The early social encyclicals did not express concern about or develop teachings on the environment. This reflects broader cultural attitudes in the West in the late nineteenth and early twentieth centuries.

As the environmental movement began to develop in a secular context in the 1950s and 1960s, an environmental ethic began to develop in the Catholic social tradition as well as in other faith traditions. The first Earth Day, in 1970, marked an important moment in the modern environment movement because it gained widespread media attention and bipartisan political support that led to the creation

Lynn White's Challenge to Christianity

In 1967, historian Lynn White published an influential essay in which he argued that the Christian tradition was largely responsible for the current environmental crisis. He argued that two features of Christian belief were particularly detrimental to the development of Western thought: an anthropocentric (human centered) view of the world and an instrumentalist view of nature, which understands the value of nature in terms of its usefulness to human beings.[1] His thought-provoking reading of Christian biblical and theological traditions has challenged many Christian ethicists and theologians to articulate a Christian response to the environmental crisis.

of the United States Environmental Protection Agency.[2] The following year, Pope Paul VI noted in *Octogesima adveniens* (*A Call to Action*, 1971), the growing awareness of environmental degradation as a moral problem, "Man is suddenly becoming aware that by an ill-considered exploitation of nature he risks destroying it and becoming in his turn the victim of this degradation" (no. 21). By identifying environmental degradation as a new social problem, Paul VI places the principle of care for creation on the agenda of CST.

The 1971 synod of bishops took up issues of justice and continued the pope's concern for the consequences of human activity on the environment. The synod's statement, *Justice in the World* (*JW*) explicitly connects the pursuit of international solidarity with the care for creation. The bishops observed that people throughout the world were becoming increasingly interconnected through advances in modern technology and the global economy. Because the earth's

---

1. Lynne White Jr., "The Historical Roots of the Environmental Crisis," *Science* (1967): 1203–7.

2. For a history of Earth Day, visit the Earth Day Network's website at *www. earthday.org.*

resources sustain human life, caring for them contributes to the common good and provides an impetus to develop global solidarity. The bishops note,

> Moreover, people are beginning to grasp a new and more radical dimension of unity; for they perceive that their resources, as well as the precious treasures of air and water—without which there cannot be life—and the small delicate biosphere of the whole complex of all life on earth, are not infinite, but on the contrary must be saved and preserved as a unique patrimony belonging to all human beings. (*JW*, no. 8)

Justice in the World articulates the relationship between the care for creation and just international development by highlighting the relationship between economic inequality and environmental degradation. The synod critiques wealthy nations for overconsumption and excessive environmental pollution:

> [S]uch is the demand for resources and energy by the richer nations, whether capitalist or socialist, and such are the effects of dumping by them in the atmosphere and the sea that irreparable damage would be done to the essential elements of life on earth, such as air and water, if their high rates of consumption and pollution, which are constantly on the increase, were extended to the whole of humanity. (*JW*, no. 11)

The statements by Paul VI and the 1971 synod of bishops call people to be concerned for the environment and recognize environmental degradation as a moral issue. CST has continued since then to emphasize the link between caring for creation and insuring that all people are able to participate in the common good, a social reality that enables people to develop their God-given potential. The engagement of CST with environmental ethics was greatly enhanced by the work of Pope John Paul II, elected to the papacy in 1978, who drew on Catholic theological sources and ethical values to develop the principle of the care for creation and to integrate it into the larger framework of CST. His successor, Pope Benedict XVI, continued that task.

Popes John Paul II and Benedict XVI on the Care for Creation

Pope John Paul II integrated the care for creation into CST by highlighting ways that environmental degradation harms people, especially those who are poor. John Paul II stressed ways that environmental destruction disproportionately impacts impoverished and marginalized communities in his 1990 World Day of Peace message *Peace with God the Creator, Peace with All of Creation* (*PGC*). He argued that the environmental crisis is related to the injustices of poverty and war. He suggests that unjust land distribution and a lack of choices to promote sustainable farming can lead to uncontrolled deforestation. Modern warfare harms ecosystems on massive levels, polluting water and soil and destroying resources. The pope emphasized that addressing the ecological crisis requires a deep commitment to global solidarity, a commitment rooted in recognizing that the consumption patterns of industrialized nations are overburdening developing countries with environmental hazards. Within this perspective, global solidarity promotes peace and human development, which are essential for the adequate care for creation.

> When the ecological crisis is set within the broader context of *the search for peace* within society, we can understand better the importance of giving attention to what the earth and its atmosphere are telling us: namely, that there is an order in the universe which must be respected, and that the human person, endowed with the capability of choosing freely, has a grave responsibility to preserve this order for the well-being of future generations. I wish to repeat that *the ecological crisis is a moral issue.* (*PGC*, no.15)

By naming the ecological crisis a moral issue, John Paul II reminded Catholics of "their serious obligation to care for all of creation" (*PGC*, no. 16).

One of the ways John Paul II challenged Catholics to carry out their moral obligation toward the environment is through resisting excessive materialism. In *Evangelium vitae* (*The Gospel of Life*, 1995), he argues that modern industrial societies suffer from an impoverished attitude toward life that is perpetuated by a consumer-driven culture that values *having* over *being*. The care for creation, from John Paul II's perspective, requires a cultural transformation that will eliminate extreme materialism and individualism characteristic of a consumer-driven culture. This transformation must be promoted through lifestyle changes that reflect a concern for the common good and a commitment to simplicity and moderation. He states,

> Modern society will find no solution to the ecological problem unless it *takes a serious look at its life style*. In many parts of the world society is given to instant gratification and consumerism while remaining indifferent to the damage which these cause. . . . If an appreciation of the value of the human person and of human life is lacking, we will also lose interest in others and in the earth itself. Simplicity, moderation and discipline, as well as the spirit of sacrifice, must become a part of everyday life, lest all suffer the negative consequences of the careless habits of a few. (*PGC*, no. 13)

Pope Benedict XVI continued the work of his predecessor, John Paul II, in many ways. In his 2009 social encyclical, *Caritas in veritate* (*Charity in Truth*) Benedict XVI identifies the connection between consumerism and the degradation of the environment (no. 51). Writing on the topic of human development in the midst of a global economic crisis, Benedict XVI's social encyclical critiques modern economic models that value efficiency and profit over the demands of solidarity. In this context, solidarity requires a more just distribution of resources among wealthy and impoverished nations with a mindfulness of the needs of future generations. Specifically, in *Caritas in veritate* (*CV*), Benedict challenges wealthy industrialized nations to lower their energy consumption and look for alternative forms of renewable energy (no. 49). The logic of his environmental ethic lies in the pope's conviction that resources should be shared among all people because "the environment is God's gift to everyone" (*CV*, no. 48).

Benedict XVI, like John Paul II, approaches environmental ethics with particular attention to the human person. He has cautioned

Green Initiatives at the Vatican

When it came to caring for the earth during his papacy, Pope Benedict XVI acted out of his convictions in public ways. In 2007 he announced his intention to make Vatican City the first carbon neutral nation in the world. The Vatican started a tree farm in Hungary to absorb as much carbon dioxide as Vatican City produces each year. In addition, the Vatican has installed rooftop solar panels to reduce its use of nonrenewable energy.[3]

against approaches to the environment that deny the dignity of the human person and the legitimacy of human needs. At the same time, he argues,

> It is also necessary to reject the opposite position, which aims at total technical dominion over nature, because the natural environment is more than raw material to be manipulated at our pleasure; it is a wondrous work of the Creator containing a 'grammar' which sets forth ends and criteria for its wise use, not its reckless exploitation. (*CV*, no. 48)

For Benedict XVI the same natural law observable in the created world provides guidelines for how people should treat each other as well as how people should treat creation (*CV*, no. 51).

The United States Conference of Catholic Bishops on the Environment

This section will focus on the USCCB's teaching on the principle of care for creation and its application of the principle to specific ecological issues by exploring two letters: *Renewing the Earth:*

---

3. Elizabeth Rosenthal, "Vatican Penance: Forgive Us Our Carbon Output," *New York Times* (September 17, 2007).

An Invitation to Reflection and Action on Environment in Light of Catholic Social Teaching (1991) and *Global Climate Change: A Plea for Dialogue, Prudence and the Common Good* (2001). Regional bishops' conferences have addressed specific environmental issues by applying the care for creation to their own contexts. This section will highlight one example—a statement by the bishops of the Northwest on the environmental issues surrounding the Columbia River watershed.

Renewing the Earth: Application of Catholic Social Teaching

Following Pope John Paul II's 1990 challenge to all Catholics to assume a moral responsibility for the environment, the USCCB issued a pastoral letter, *Renewing the Earth*. The bishops explain that the intent of the letter is to highlight the moral dimensions of the environmental crisis, particularly with respect to the poor and vulnerable, and to provide a religious perspective on ecological responsibility.

The bishops ground their position in CST. Specifically, in *Renewing the Earth* (no. 27) they list the following guidelines for their environmental ethic:

- *a God-centered and sacramental view of the universe*, which grounds human accountability for the fate of the earth;
- a consistent *respect for human life*, which extends to respect for all creation;
- a worldview affirming the ethical significance of *global interdependence and the common good;*
- *an ethic of solidarity* promoting cooperation and a just structure of sharing in the world community;
- an understanding of *the universal purpose of created things*, which requires equitable use of the earth's resources;
- *an option for the poor*, which gives passion to the quest for an equitable and sustainable world;
- a conception of *authentic development*, which offers a direction for progress that respects human dignity and the limits of material growth.

The first theme requires some elaboration as it provides the theological foundation for the bishops' position. A sacramental view of the universe presupposes that God is revealed through the created world. Catholic thought and practice emphasize the notion that the presence of God is mediated through tangible objects and rituals in a number of ways. This is exemplified in the seven sacraments the Catholic Church celebrates—baptism, confirmation, marriage, ordination, Eucharist, reconciliation, and anointing of the sick. Each of these rituals incorporates material elements and gestures to communicate a mystery of the Christian faith. The foundational belief behind the sacraments is that the physical world communicates God's invisible presence.

The bishops draw on the theological understanding of sacrament because experiencing God in the material aspect of the sacraments may also promote a reverence for all nonhuman creation, as it potentially reveals God's presence in the world. The bishops draw on the concept of sacrament to emphasize the value of creation by affirming the intrinsic value of nonhuman life. This provides a basis for the care for creation. The bishops state in *Renewing the Earth* (*RE*), "The diversity of life manifests God's glory. . . . Accordingly, it is appropriate that we treat other creatures and the natural world not just as means to human fulfillment but also as God's creatures, possessing an independent value, worthy of respect and care" (no. 34).

The sacramental view of the world places God at the center of creation and has implications on how people should relate to the natural world. The bishops suggest, "Dwelling in the presence of God, we begin to experience ourselves as part of creation, as stewards within it, not separate from it" (*RE*, no. 31). They elaborate on their understanding of stewardship in the text. As stewards of creation, they argue, people are not free to use the earth's resources indiscriminately but should follow ethical guidelines for responsible management. Stewardship, they note, requires balancing human needs with the needs of the natural world.

While affirming the value of nonhuman life, the USCCB does not let go of the unique dignity of the human person. They do, however, recognize the potential tension between affirming the dignity of the human person and recognizing that humans exist within, not above, creation. The bishops invite Catholic theologians, Scripture

The Meaning of Stewardship

A steward is entrusted with responsibility for something that belongs to a higher authority. Christians have used the concept of stewardship to emphasize responsibility toward creation out of recognition of that it belongs to God. The concept has helped Christians interpret the Genesis account of Creation that instructs humans to have dominion over the earth (1:28). Environmentalists decry the effect of interpretations of this passage that suggest that people have unlimited authority over creation. Understanding the concept of *dominion* within the historical context of the Hebrew Bible, some scholars suggest that dominion has less to do with control and domination and more to do with establishing human connection to nature and mandating human responsibility toward it.[4] Even within this interpretation, environmentalists and ethicists within and outside of Christianity have critiqued the stewardship approach to ecology for not adequately demonstrating the interdependence of humanity and creation.[5]

scholars, and ethicists to "explore the relationship between this [the Catholic] tradition's emphasis on the dignity of the human person and our responsibility to care for all of God's creation" (*RE*, no. 71).

Renewing the Earth: Social Justice and the Environment

In *Renewing the Earth*, the USCCB highlights the relationship between social justice and the care for creation. Specifically, they draw on the long-standing Catholic social principles of solidarity

---

4. For example, see Anne Clifford, "Foundations for a Catholic Ecological Theology of God," in *And God Saw That It Was Good: Catholic Theology and the Environment*, eds. Drew Christiansen and Walter Grazer (Washington, DC: USCCB, 1996), 22–28.

5. For example, see Elizabeth Johnson, *Women, Earth, and Creator Spirit* (New York: Paulist Press, 1993) who argues for a kinship model that expresses the relationship between human and nonhuman life in familial terms.

and the common good to frame human responsibility toward the environment. The bishops suggest that the ecological crisis presents an urgent opportunity to recognize "just how interdependent our world is" (*RE*, no. 36). Because all of humanity is affected by the abuse of the earth and overuse of the earth's resources, the environmental crisis transcends human divisions of culture, nationality, race, and ethnicity. At the same time, as the bishops have stressed, the environmental crisis affects groups in different ways. People in developing countries are harmed by environmental hazards and over-consumption of the earth's resources more than people living in other parts of the world. Solidarity, in the face of such disparity, becomes a foundational principle behind environmental justice because it invites Christians in wealthier nations to correct this disparity. The bishops argue that solidarity places particular demands on wealthy, industrialized countries like the United States, which might require "sacrifices of our own self-interest for the good of others and of the earth we share" (*RE*, no. 39).

A focal point of the bishops' work on the environment has been the intersection of ecological degradation, poverty, and racism. They explicitly point out the connection between the environment and economic justice:

> The whole human race suffers as a result of environmental blight, and generations yet unborn will bear the cost for our failure to act today. But in most countries today, including our own, it is the poor and the powerless who most directly bear the burden of current environmental carelessness. Their lands and neighborhoods are more likely to be polluted or to host toxic waste dumps, their water to be undrinkable, their children to be harmed. Too often, the structure of sacrifice involved in environmental remedies seems to exact a high price from the poor and from workers. (*RE*, no. 7)

By focusing on the human dimension of the environmental crisis—how it diminishes human life and perpetuates inequalities between the rich and the poor—the bishops are able to make solid connections between the care for creation and other principles of CST. In particular, the USCCB's discussion of environmental ethics consistently reflects the Catholic Church's commitment to human dignity, the common good, and the option for the poor.

Promoting environmental justice relates to the Catholic Church's defense of the poor and vision of authentic human development. The bishops refer to the foundational work of Pope Paul VI, stressing that the Catholic Church considers human development not only in terms of economic growth but also in terms of the social, spiritual, and moral development of a person. The bishops state, "Catholic social teaching has never accepted material growth as a model of development. . . . Authentic development supports moderation and even austerity in the use of material resources" (*RE*, nos. 45, 46). This understanding of development is conducive to promoting balance between economic growth and the care for creation. Within the vision of development offered by Catholic social thought, the accumulation of material goods is not the sole indicator of human flourishing. Rather, integral development relates to the cultural, moral, and spiritual well-being of a person and community.

Global Climate Change

In recent years, the USCCB has been vocal about the need for an immediate response to a specific environmental concern—climate change. They point to a growing consensus in the scientific community that the earth's temperatures are changing at an alarming rate, causing a number of environmental hazards, such as floods, erosion of coastal lands, and loss of biodiversity. Scientists understand the primary cause of this rapid change to be a result of carbon emissions from human activities: industry, transportation, and deforestation.[6] The issue of climate change has become contentious within the United States, with political debates on the threat of global climate change and the ways to address it.[7] In their 2001 statement, *Global Climate Change: A Plea for Dialogue, Prudence and the Common Good*

---

6. Center for Climate and Energy Solutions, available online *http://www.pewclimate.org/global-warming-basics/about*.

7. For information on the public debates, see Frans Berkhout, "Constructing Boundaries and Reason in the Climate Debate," *Global Environmental Change* Vol. 20, Issue 4 (October 2010): 565–69.

(*GCC*), the USCCB focuses the reader's attention beyond the political debates to the moral issue of environmental responsibility:

> At its core, global climate change is not about economic theory or political platforms, nor about partisan advantage or interest group pressures. It is about the future of God's creation and the one human family. It is about protecting both "the human environment" and the natural environment. It is about our human stewardship of God's creation and our responsibility to those who come after us. (*GCC*, no. 3)

In the text, the bishops draw on CST to address the issue of climate change, appealing to the common good and an ethic of solidarity. The bishops challenge environmentalists who identify overpopulation in developing countries as a central cause of global climate change. The bishops invite the reader to focus, instead, on the problems of materialism and consumption in developed countries:

> The global climate change debate cannot become just another opportunity for some groups—usually affluent advocates from the developed nations—to blame the problem on population growth in poor countries. Historically, the industrialized countries have emitted more greenhouse gases that warm the climate than have the developing countries. Affluent nations such as our own have to acknowledge the impact of voracious consumerism instead of simply calling for population and emission controls from people in poorer nations. (*GCC*, no. 22)

The USCCB's emphasis on curbing consumption rather than population control reflects the teachings of Popes John Paul II and Benedict XVI on the environment.

The Bishops of the Northwest on the Columbia River Watershed

Unlike climate change, which impacts the entire globe, some environmental issues are specific to particular regions and require a more local response. Regional groups of bishops have addressed such issues in the United States. The bishops of New England, New Mexico, Alaska, and Florida have made statements on specific environmental issues impacting their churches. One of the best examples of collaboration among regional bishops can be observed in the statement on the Columbia River watershed.

Building on principles laid out in *Renewing the Earth*, a group of bishops from the Pacific Northwest[8] wrote a pastoral letter in 2000 on the ethical dimensions surrounding the Columbia River watershed. Specifically, they raise concern about the impact of logging, mining, and fishing on the watershed's ecosystem. At the same time, they recognize how important these industries are to local residents. In their letter, they reflect on the challenge of balancing human needs with the proper care for the earth. They begin their reflection by stating that "the watershed is ultimately God's; human beings are entrusted with responsibility for it, concern for its species and ecology, and regulation of its competitive and complementary uses."[9] The writers recognize that industries such as fishing, logging, and mining have been important sources of livelihood to the residents of the Northwest, and they also recognize that these industries have been sources of ecological damage in the area. For this reason, the bishops recognize the tensions that emerge between landowners, workers, and environmental groups. Observing this tension, the bishops call for "a thorough, humble and introspective evaluation that seeks to eliminate both economic greed that fails to respect the environment, and ecological elitism that lacks a proper regard for the legitimate rights and property of others."[10]

The northwestern bishops highlight a prominent theme in CST on the environment in their concern for human needs in relation to the environment. The Columbia River watershed provides just one example of how resource management and conservation can exist in tension with people's jobs and interests. In response, the bishops

8. This includes bishops from Washington, Oregon, Montana, Idaho, and British Columbia.

9. Columbia River Pastoral Letter Project, "The Columbia Watershed: Caring for Creation and the Common Good," (2000) available online at *http://thewscc.org/index. php?option=com_content&view=article&id=38&Itemid=67.*

10. Ibid., 2.

invite dialogue on how to balance the immediate interests and needs of people with long-term planning on care for the environment.

Reading the Signs of the Times: Environmental Racism

This section will further discuss the disproportionate impact of environmental harm on racial minorities. Identified as environmental racism, this is a significant moral issue in the United States today.

Environmental racism names a connection between institutionalized discrimination and the degradation of the environment. Sociologist Robert Bullard suggests "environmental racism refers to environmental policies, practices, or directives that differentially affect or disadvantage (whether intentionally or unintentionally) individuals, groups, or communities based on race or color."[11] Environmental racism is perpetuated by social structures and attitudes that discriminate against racial minorities. It can be observed on domestic and international levels. The growing influence of multinational corporations in the global economy has left developing nations vulnerable to environmental exploitation. As developing nations compete with each other to cater to corporate interests, environmental standards can suffer. Race is a notable factor in this reality, as the most economically impoverished countries tend to be inhabited by indigenous populations and people of color.[12]

Environmental racism is also a problem within the United States, despite the presence of an Environmental Protection Agency that implements national environmental protection laws aimed to keep a standard level of safety and health for all citizens. Even when environmental regulations are in place, communities may experience different levels of enforcement of those protections. Studies have shown that people of color and low-income communities in the United States experience less environmental protection than majority white communities. Industries dispose of more waste and emit

---

11. Robert Bullard, "Confronting Environmental Racism in the Twenty-First Century," *Global Dialogue* Vol. 4, Issue 1 (Winter 2002): 2.
12. Ibid.

more toxins near predominantly minority communities than near predominantly white communities, which tend to have more economic and political power.[13]

Racism is a factor in environmental degradation in both rural and urban areas of the United States. For example, in 2007 scholars working with the Center for Justice, Tolerance, and Peace at the University of California–Santa Cruz documented levels of environmental hazards by regions in the San Francisco Bay area. The researchers identified numerous correlations between social inequalities and environmental hazards. They found that racial minorities were more likely than white people to live in close proximity to a toxic release facility. Specifically, African Americans are three times more likely than whites to live within one mile of a toxic release facility, and although income was a factor in the disparities they measured, African Americans at all income levels were still more likely than whites to live near the toxic release sites.[14] The researchers concluded,

> This study demonstrates that the Bay Area is also characterized by an unequal distribution of our environmental burdens and opportunities—and no amount of sophisticated statistical attempts to control for other factors seems to erase the stain of racial and economic inequality.[15]

The reality of environmental racism demonstrates the connection between social justice and environmental justice, a theme that is strongly developed in Catholic social thought since the late 1970s. Walter Grazer, writing as the director of the USCCB's Environmental Justice Program, identifies the integration of social justice and the care for creation as a primary challenge for the Catholic Church. According to Grazer, such integration requires listening to marginalized voices, "We must find a way to give expression to the voices, needs and hurts of the poor and vulnerable if we are to integrate the

---

13. Robert Bullard, Paul Mohai, Robin Saha, and Beverly Wright, "Toxic Wastes and Race at Twenty" *Environmental Law*, Vol. 38, Issue 2 (Spring 2008): 371–411.

14. Manual Pastor, James Sadd, and Rachel Morello-Frosch, "Still Toxic After All These Years: Air Quality and Environmental Justice in the San Francisco Bay Area," (2007) available online at *http://cjtc.ucsc.edu/docs/bay_final.pdf.*

15. Ibid., 14.

search for social justice and environmental wholeness."[16] He goes on to identify specific ways that the US Catholic community is making an effort to place the needs of people living in poverty at the center of environmental justice programs. For example, Catholic Charities USA trains low-income families to avoid exposure to household toxins and the Catholic Campaign for Human Development advocates for farmers who are exposed to harmful pesticides on the job.[17]

Summary and Integration for Service Learners

The Catholic Church's teaching on the care for creation reveals a concern for how environmental destruction affects human life, particularly the lives of the most vulnerable. For both Pope John Paul II and Pope Benedict XVI, the care for creation is understood in light of other Catholic social principles, particularly solidarity, the common good, and human dignity. Their teachings challenge wealthy individuals and nations to consider the effect of overconsumption on people and nations suffering from poverty. This option for the poor and vulnerable is a central principle underlying the Catholic Church's teachings about the need to bring justice to people suffering from environmental racism.

The USCCB links social justice with their approach to the environment, emphasizing the human suffering caused by environmental destruction. They have articulated the intrinsic value of creation and have invited Catholics to practice care for the environment as an aspect of their faith. The current challenge for CST on the environment was summarized in the USCCB's invitation to theologians, biblical scholars, and ethicists to continue to reflect on the relationship between human dignity and the care for creation (*RE*, no. 71).

Now that you have read about the principle of care for creation articulated in CST, revisit your responses to the questions at the beginning of the chapter. Would you answer any questions differently? Does the chapter's discussion about environmental degradation and its

---

16. Walter Grazer, "Environmental Justice: A Catholic Voice," *America* Vol. 190, Issue 2 (January 19, 2004): 15.

17. Ibid., 13.

connection to racism shed light on social issues you've encountered in a service-leaning setting? Use the following vignette and questions to practice aspects of the see-judge-act process in relation to this topic.

Where Does My Garbage End Up?

Service-Learning Vignette

A student serving at a community garden noticed a bad smell in the air that would intensify when the temperature rose. On further investigation, she discovered that the city dump was located in close proximity to the neighborhood and was causing the air to smell like garbage. The garden is located in a low-income neighborhood whose residents are predominantly Asian and African American. The student, who lives in a predominantly white middle-class neighborhood in the same city said that she has never thought about where her garbage ended up, and she just assumed that it would be far away from people's homes.

See: Social Analysis

- How might environmental racism have contributed to the situation described in the vignette?
- What information would help you assess the extent to which racial discrimination may have contributed to the close proximity of the city dump and the neighborhood where the garden is located?

Judge: Ethical Reflection

- How might the Catholic social principles of the preferential option for the poor, solidarity, and the care for creation apply to the situation described in the vignette?
- How does the US bishops' invitation to consider the relationship between the unique dignity of the person and the care for creation relate to the situation described in the vignette?

Act: Promoting Justice

- Identify actions aligned with CST's calls to care for creation and protect the dignity of human beings that might help to prevent environmental racism.

- Identify any attitudes, policies, and institutions that you are aware of that, according to CST, should be challenged in order to address disparities in the enforcement of environmental protections.

Suggestions for Further Social Analysis in a Service-Learning Context

- Gather data on environmental hazards and the racial and socioeconomic demographics in three or more neighborhoods or communities in a selected city. Does the data suggest any correlation between the number and types of hazards and the race or socioeconomic status of the people in the neighborhoods?
- Research the debates about global climate change. How do the various positions you encounter relate to environmental policies?
- Investigate the availability of green lifestyle options (e.g., recycling, composting, organic and biodegradable products, sustainable energy sources) in a selected neighborhood or city. Compare these findings with the availability of such options in other areas. If you find differences, consider what might contribute to them.

For Further Reading on Catholic Social Thought on the Environment

Christiansen, Drew, and Walter Grazer, eds. *And God Saw That It Was Good: Catholic Theology and the Environment*. Washington, DC: USCCB, 1996.

Miller, Richard, ed. *God, Creation, and Climate Change: A Catholic Response to the Environmental Crisis*. Maryknoll, NY: Orbis, 2010.

Nothwehr, Dawn. *Ecological Footprints: An Essential Franciscan Guide for Faith and Sustainable Living*. Collegeville, MN: Liturgical Press, 2012.

Schaefer, Jame. *Confronting the Climate Crisis: Catholic Theological Perspectives*. Milwaukee: Marquette University Press, 2011.

Winright, Tobias, ed. *Green Discipleship: Catholic Theological Ethics and the Environment*. Winona, MN: Anselm Academic, 2011.

Rights and Responsibilities in a Globalized Context

Introduction

The Catholic social tradition affirms that the dignity of human beings can be safeguarded only if the rights of individuals are protected. Demonstrating a strong commitment to the common good, the Catholic Church has promoted a distinctive approach to human rights, which affirms the social nature of the person and the importance of solidarity. For this reason, Catholic social teaching (CST) discusses rights alongside responsibilities. The principle of rights and responsibilities communicates a foundational commitment of the Catholic social tradition—to protect the dignity of the individual and the good of a community at the same time. Reflect on your understanding of human rights and responsibilities and, if possible, relate this understanding to service-learning settings with which you may be familiar.

- What is the meaning of *human rights?* What rights are universal? What experiences, ideas, and values have shaped your understanding of human rights?
- How do you understand your responsibility to the communities with which you identify most immediately (family, neighborhood, university) and then more broadly (city, nation, world)? How do you understand your responsibility to communities you may be familiar with through service learning?
- How are rights to private property, health care, and education protected within the context of a service-learning setting with which you are familiar and within the broader community

where that setting is located? Does everyone have access to these resources? If not, what limits a person's access to these resources?

The protection of human rights and the carrying out of responsibilities is affected by globalization, which describes multiple features of the contemporary world. Sociologists David Held and Andrew McGrew offer a helpful definition, "globalization denotes the expanding scale, growing magnitude, speeding up and deepening impact of interregional flows and patterns of social interaction."[1] There are many economic, political, and cultural implications of globalization that raise ethical questions. This chapter focuses on economic globalization, which is characterized by the flow of goods, services, and technology across borders and the interdependence between national economies. Consider the meaning and significance of economic globalization and, if possible, relate these ideas to a service-learning setting with which you are familiar.

- What are some benefits of economic globalization? What are some of its harmful effects? Have you experienced any of the benefits or harms? Have people you may know through service learning been affected by economic globalization. If so, how?

- Who are the major actors behind economic globalization? Do certain groups of people tend to hold power that helps to direct globalization? If so, who, and what is the source of their power? What social structures would need to be analyzed to understand better the power dynamics behind globalization?

- Identify local organizations that work to meet the needs of the poor, and consider how their efforts relate to globalization. Do these efforts suggest some specific ways that local initiatives can contribute to worldwide change?

This chapter will explore the development of the principle of the rights and responsibilities in CST and examine how the United

---

1. David Held and Andrew McGrew, "The Great Globalization Debate," in *The Global Transformations Reader: An Introduction to the Globalization Debate*, eds. David Held and Andrew McGrew (Malden MA: Blackwell/Polity Press, 2004), 4.

States Conference of Catholic Bishops (USCCB) has applied this principle in response to issues raised by economic globalization, focusing on two of their statements, *Called to Global Solidarity: International Challenges for US Parishes* (1997) and *A Place at the Table* (2002). It will also highlight how the bishops have implemented these teachings through the work of Catholic Relief Services and the Catholics Confront Global Poverty campaign. Next, the chapter will draw on insights from Christian ethics to help service learners begin to analyze globalization and assess its effects. The final section of the chapter provides a summary followed by a vignette drawn from an actual service-learning setting and a series of questions designed to help readers become more familiar with the see-judge-act process.

Catholic Social Teaching on Rights and Responsibilities

Rights and Duties in the Early Social Encyclicals

The Catholic Church's position on human rights has developed over time and is best understood within the context out of which it emerged. In 1864, Pope Pius IX issued a *Syllabus of Errors*, in which he explicitly rejected characteristic features of modernity, including the right to religious liberty and the right to freedom of speech.[2] The pope associated these rights with modernity, the Enlightenment, and the French Revolution, all of which he considered to be threats to the Catholic Church's authority. The pope and many of his contemporaries feared that the Enlightenment's emphasis on human reason and individual freedoms were incompatible with the Church's emphasis on the social nature of the person, the authority of the church, and the objectivity of moral truth. This reactionary approach to the Western tradition of human rights influenced Catholic thought until the Second Vatican Council.[3]

---

2. Pope Pius IX, *Quanta Cura and Syllabus of Errors* (1864) nos. 15, 79 (Kansas City: Angelus Press, 1998).

3. Drew Christiansen, "Commentary on *Pacem in Terris* (*Peace on Earth*)" in *Modern Catholic Social Teaching*, eds. Himes, et al. (Washington, DC: Georgetown University Press, 2005), 224.

The early social encyclicals (1891–1931) of Popes Leo XIII and Pius XI moved beyond Pius IX's rigid condemnation of modernity. Both popes defended the natural right to private property in an effort to argue against socialism. They also argued that a person's right to private property is not absolute: it is limited by the person's duty or responsibility to promote the common good. By emphasizing duties alongside rights, the early social encyclicals rejected what they saw as the dangers of Enlightenment thinking—individualism and unlimited freedom—without rejecting all features of modernity.

Pope John XXIII and the Catholic Human Rights Tradition

Pope John XXIII was instrumental in integrating the discussion of specific human rights into the Catholic Church's official social teaching. He articulated a vision of human rights in his social encyclical, *Pacem in terris* (*Peace on Earth*, 1963), an encyclical that made a significant contribution to the Catholic human rights tradition. Social ethicist, David Hollenbach argues that "*Pacem in terris* moved the leadership of the Church from a position of staunch opposition to modern rights and freedoms to activist engagement in the global struggle for human rights. This shift was one of the most dramatic reversals in the long history of the Catholic tradition."[4] *Pacem in terris* (*PT*) was the first major papal writing to be addressed to the whole world, not just Catholics. The universal audience of the encyclical reflects the universal scope of its content. John XXIII articulated an awareness of the growing interdependence of people throughout the world and argued for universal human rights out of the recognition of that interdependence. The pope expressed his support for the United Nations 1948 *Universal Declaration of Human Rights* (*PT*, nos. 143–44) and echoed many of the declaration's themes.

John XXIII grounds his argument for universal human rights in natural law, appealing to an understanding of human nature reflected in the Catholic teaching. He begins with the conviction,

---

4. David Hollenbach, "Commentary on *Gaudium et Spes*," in *Modern Catholic Social Teaching*, eds. Himes, et al. (Washington, DC: Georgetown University Press, 2005), 280.

> Any well-regulated and productive association of men in
> society demands the acceptance of one fundamental prin-
> ciple: that each individual man is truly a person. His is a
> nature, that is, endowed with intelligence and free will.
> As such he has rights and duties, which together flow as a
> direct consequence from his nature. (*PT*, no. 9)

John XXIII offers a person-centered understanding of rights, emphasizing the dignity of the human person rooted in the human qualities
of rationality and free will. Within this perspective, rights and responsibilities flow from human existence not from specific actions or ideas.
Grounded in human dignity, human rights are intrinsic and universal,
not earned or granted to a person based on certain conditions.

Continuing the Catholic social tradition's emphasis on the call
to community and the common good, John XXIII describes human
rights as protected by social life. The rights listed in *Pacem in terris*
include the basic necessities for human life such as food, shelter, and
medical care, as well as rights that enable people to participate fully
in the life of a society—education, participation in political life, and
freedom to worship God according to one's conscience. Affirming
that rights are always realized in the context of community, John
lists individual rights, along with corresponding duties to support
the rights of others and protect the common good. For example, the
right to life involves the duty to preserve life; the right to freedom of
conscience carries the duty to seek the truth (*PT*, no. 9).

Popes Paul VI and John Paul II: Solidarity and Human Rights

Papal teaching after Vatican II reflects a strong commitment to
human rights and consistently speaks about these rights in connection to responsibilities toward the community. In *Populorum progressio* (*The Development of Peoples*, 1967), Pope Paul VI emphasized
the relationship between rights and responsibilities. In *Populorum
progressio* (*PP*), he expresses his views on private property: ". . . the
right to private property is not absolute or unconditional. No one
may appropriate surplus goods solely for his own private use when
others lack the bare necessities of life" (no. 23). Paul VI continues

the Catholic social tradition's insistence on the universal purpose of created things to stress that the right to private property is a limited right. Writing with an awareness of severe economic inequalities, Paul VI argued that responsibility for the common good sets limits on a person's right to accumulate wealth. For example, the pope criticizes wealthy individuals who hoard their money through foreign investments rather than giving back to their local community (*PP*, no. 24). In the face of growing inequalities between nations, Paul VI calls wealthier countries to solidarity with developing countries.

In his 1987 social encyclical *Sollicitudo rei socialis* (*On Social Concern*), Pope John Paul II follows Paul VI's call for solidarity in response to the increasingly inequitable distribution of resources throughout the world. In *Sollicitudo rei socialis* (*SRS*), he argues for just distribution of goods out of a spirit of international solidarity.

> It is necessary to state once more the characteristic principle of Christian social doctrine: the goods of this world are originally meant for all. The right to private property is valid and necessary, but it does not nullify the value of this principle. Private property, in fact, is under a "social mortgage," which means that it has an intrinsically social function, based on and justified precisely by the principle of the universal destination of goods. (No. 42)

John Paul II highlights the meaning of rights and responsibilities in his understanding of private property. Because creation is intended for the benefit of all, one cannot legitimately hoard a surplus of goods while others are lacking basic necessities. The pope observes an unjust distribution of goods in the international community and identifies some specific problems with the global economy that perpetuate such injustice. He argues that international trade systems disadvantage developing countries by devaluing their raw materials. He also notes that multinational companies take advantage of low-cost labor in some countries without ensuring fair labor laws (*SRS*, no. 43). The pope invites a reexamination of international systems that regulate finance and exchange, arguing that they have failed to promote the development of all nations (*SRS*, no. 43). He proposes collaboration among nations to secure the rights of everyone.

Pope Benedict XVI on Globalization and Human Rights

In his 2009 message for World Peace Day, Pope Benedict XVI addressed the challenge of ameliorating human rights violations and injustices, which contribute to the marginalization of the poor throughout the world:

> Globalization eliminates certain barriers, but is still able to build new ones; it brings peoples together, but spatial and temporal proximity does not of itself create the conditions for true communion and authentic peace. Effective means to redress the marginalization of the world's poor through globalization will only be found if people everywhere feel personally outraged by the injustices in the world and by the concomitant violations of human rights.[5]

In his social encyclical, *Caritas in veritate* (*Charity in Truth*, 2009), Benedict XVI offers a strong critique of the trends in economic globalization that trample the rights of the poor. In *Caritas in veritate* (*CV*), Benedict XVII argues for a global ethic based on the virtue of gratuitousness, through which all people would recognize the goods of creation as gifts to be shared. The notion of gratuitousness counteracts current driving forces of the market—consumerism and competition. Benedict XVI argues that gratuitousness fosters solidarity, and that solidarity is badly needed in a globalized economy that too often suppresses the poor (*CV*, nos. 34–35).

Benedict XVI also makes the point that "the economic sphere is neither ethically neutral, nor inherently inhuman and opposed to society. It is part and parcel of human activity and precisely because it is human, it must be structured and governed in an ethical manner" (*CV*, no. 36). Benedict XVI regards globalization in a similar way—it is not inherently good or bad but should be directed to the service of humanity. He states,

> As a human reality, it [globalization] is the product of diverse cultural tendencies, which need to be subjected to a process

---

5. Pope Benedict XVI, "Fighting Poverty to Build Peace," Message on the 2009 World Day of Peace, no. 8, available online at *http://www.vatican.va/holy_father/ benedict_xvi/messages/peace/documents/hf_ben-xvi_mes_20081208_xlii-world-day-peace_en.html.*

of discernment. The truth of globalization as a process and its fundamental ethical criterion are given by the unity of the human family and its development towards what is good. Hence a sustained commitment is needed so as to *promote a person-based and community-oriented cultural process of world-wide integration that is open to transcendence.* (*CV*, no. 42)

Emphasizing the unity of the human family, the pope stresses the importance of solidarity in directing the process of economic global-ization. The principle of rights and responsibilities can also be seen throughout the text. The pope argues that an individual's economic rights carry responsibilities toward the flourishing of the whole com-munity. As the world's inhabitants become increasingly interconnected through the process of globalization, human flourishing takes on a global dimension. In order to direct economic globalization toward human flourishing, Benedict XVI argues for the cooperation between nations as well as the establishment of an international authority to ensure democratic oversight of the global economy (*CV*, no. 41).

The Vatican Calls for Corporate Responsibility

In 2012, the Pontifical Council for Justice and Peace issued a statement entitled, "The Vocation of the Business Leader: A Reflection." The reflection is presented as a resource to help business leaders connect their work to Christian values. Follow-ing the model of *see-judge-act,* the text invites business leaders to (1) observe the challenges and opportunities for promoting economic justice through their work, (2) to judge their observa-tions in light of the principles of human dignity and the common good, and (3) to act on behalf of justice in their vocation, connect-ing their faith to their career in business leadership.[6]

---

6. Pontifical Council for Justice and Peace, "The Vocation of the Business Leader: A Reflection" (2012) available online at *http://www.stthomas.edu/cathstudies/cst/conferences/Logic%20of%20Gift%20Semina/Logicofgiftdoc/FinalsoftproofVocati.pdf.*

The United States Conference of Catholic Bishops on Global Responsibility

This section will examine how the USCCB has applied the principle of rights and responsibilities to frame the US role in the international community. The work of protecting human rights and meeting responsibilities for the common good presents particular challenges and opportunities for those living in the United States. US culture, with its strong emphasis on personal freedom and the opportunity to accumulate wealth does not readily support the notion of responsibility to the common good.[7] The USCCB has consistently voiced the concern for common good against the dominant American ethos that focuses on individual rights and freedoms. Perhaps the best example of this is their approach to economic justice. Recall that in *Economic Justice for All* the bishops evaluate an economy based on how well it serves the most vulnerable people. The US bishops reiterate themes from *Economic Justice for All* in their statements on globalization. In 1996, for example, they expressed concern about the negative effect of globalization on the rights of those living in poverty:

> Because the economy has moral dimensions, economic choices and institutions must be judged by how they protect or undermine the life and dignity of the human person. As individuals, all have the right to the basic necessities of life—food, education, shelter, medical care, job security, productive work, just wages and working conditions, as well as the consequent duty to provide for our families and to contribute to society. In the globalized economy, these rights appear to be much less secure.[8]

Recognizing the connection between the protection of individual rights and meeting responsibilities to the larger community, the bishops

---

7. John Coleman, "North American Culture's Receptivity to CST" in *Catholic Social Teaching in Global Perspective*, ed. Daniel McDonald (Maryknoll, NY: Orbis, 2010), 198.

8. USCCB Office of International Justice and Peace, "The Globalized Economy: Challenges to the Church in the US" (1996) available at *http://old.usccb.org/sdwp/international/globcon96.shtml*.

emphasize the role of solidarity in responding to increasing global interconnections. This section will explore the work of the USCCB by examining two pastoral letters, *Called to Global Solidarity* and *A Place at the Table*, and two initiatives, Catholic Relief Services and Catholics Confront Global Poverty campaign, which aim to promote global solidarity and defend human rights in the context of globalization.

Called to Global Solidarity

In their 1997 statement, *Called to Global Solidarity* (*CGS*), the USCCB argues that Catholics in the United States have unique responsibilities toward the global common good because they are both members of a worldwide church and citizens of a nation with influence across the world. Speaking on behalf of US Catholics, the bishops state, "We are members of a universal Church that transcends national boundaries and calls us to live in solidarity and justice with the peoples of the world. We are also citizens of a powerful democracy with enormous influence beyond our borders" (*CGS*, no. 1). In the statement, the bishops discuss specific ways that economic globalization has widened the gap between wealthy and impoverished nations. They also note that the globalization of markets, transportation, and communication has increased people's awareness of the interconnectedness of the world. Globalization has also generated greater awareness of the injustices around the world. Specifically, the bishops note that communication technologies and global media allow the world to see images of genocide in Rwanda and Darfur and other cases of crimes against humanity. At the same time, they fear that the awareness of human rights violations has not necessarily led to efforts to eliminate such injustices. Among US citizens, the bishops suggest, "There is increasing complacency about the defense of human rights" (*CGS*, no. 11).

The USCCB insists that apathy toward global injustice contradicts the demands of the Christian faith. National leaders and large agencies are called to respond to injustice but so are individuals and local communities, the bishops explain. For example, they call on local parishes to integrate a global perspective and commitment to justice into their life and identity. "Catholic communities of faith should measure their prayer, education, and action by how they serve the life, dignity, and rights of the human person at home and abroad"

(*CGS*, no. 30). One of the ways that the USCCB has encouraged global responsibility within parishes is through connecting parishes to the Catholic Church's existing international activities. Individual Catholics are often unaware of the charity and justice work of the international Catholic community. Specifically, many Catholics do not know about the work of Catholic Relief Services.

Catholic Relief Services and the Catholics Confront Global Poverty Campaign

Catholic Relief Services (CRS), the USCCB's official international humanitarian agency, is driven by the principles of CST, promoting human dignity, the common good, and solidarity through direct service, education, and advocacy. Since the US bishops established CRS in 1943, the organization has spread throughout the world, now serving more than one hundred million people in more than one hundred countries.[9] CRS's microfinance program provides a good example of their work to empower communities living in poverty. By working with community-based saving groups or larger microfinance associations, CRS has provided loans to help low-income groups develop revenue-generating initiatives in their communities. For example, from 2000 to 2008, CRS partnered with local chickpea farmers in Tanzania to organize farmers to create a collaborative Savings and Internal Lending Community (SILC). Within the SILC model, farmers could access loans during peak farming season in order to increase their revenue. With greater revenue, they could invest their profits back into the group savings and benefit the whole group.[10]

In 2005, the USCCB and CRS developed a campaign called "Catholics Confront Global Poverty" to address international poverty by promoting just trade, debt relief, international peace through development, justice for migrants, and effective aid to impoverished countries.[11] The campaign also focuses on environmental justice,

9. Catholic Relief Services' Web site is available at *www.crs.org*.

10. Catholic Relief Services Microfinance Occasional Paper (November 2010) available online at: *http://www.crsprogramquality.org/storage/pubs/microfinance/Savings-led%20Microfinance%20in%20Tanzania.pdf*.

11. The history of Catholics Confront Global Poverty is available at *http://old.usccb.org/sdwp/globalpoverty/ccgp_history.shtml*.

seeking to promote the just extraction and distribution of natural resources and combat global climate change. The campaign specifically addresses economic globalization, critiquing liberal trade agreements and agriculture subsidies that exploit poor nations for their natural resources, agricultural products, and labor.

Free Trade vs. Fair Trade

Economic globalization is supported by the opening up of borders to increase the flow of goods and services between nations. This process has been facilitated by free trade agreements such as the 1994 North American Free Trade Agreement between Mexico, Canada, and the United States (NAFTA). Free trade agreements such as NAFTA do not necessarily result in equal benefits for all countries. The Carnegie Foundation funded a 2004 study to assess the impact of NAFTA ten years after its implementation. Researchers found that NAFTA had an overall negative impact on the Mexican economy, citing a loss of 1.3 million agriculture jobs and a drop in real wages for the majority of Mexicans since 1994.[12] One of the reasons NAFTA has been particularly hard on the rural population in Mexico, the researchers explain, is that Mexican farmers were unable to compete with large subsidized US farms that were able to sell their products at significantly lower prices.[13] The fair trade movement developed as a way to advocate for farmers in developing countries and inform consumers about the labor practices and environmental impact of the products they buy. For more information about fair trade see *www.fairtradeusa.org* and *www.globalexchange.org*.

---

12. John Audley, Demetrios Papademetriou, Sandra Polaski, and Scott Vaugh, "NAFTA's Promise and Reality: Lessons from Mexico for the Hemisphere, "Carnegie Endowment for International Peace, 2004): 6, available online at *http://carnegieendowment. org/files/nafta1.pdf.*

13. Ibid., p. 16.

The Catholics Confront Global Poverty campaign highlights the effects of globalization on human life and points out how people's decisions can mitigate the harmful effects of globalization. Global poverty and the resulting injustices—hunger, violence, the displacement of people, the exploitation of farmers and other workers, environmental degradation, and selling vulnerable girls and women to traffickers who promise decent wages and a better life in another country—are not inevitable. The campaign stresses the unrealized influence of the global Catholic community to promote economic justice in the context of globalization. Therefore, it seeks to educate and mobilize one million Catholics to act out of solidarity with the poor and vulnerable.[14]

A Place at the Table

Although the USCCB implores Catholics to take responsibility for the alleviation of poverty, they argue that all people share in the responsibility. In a 2002 pastoral statement, *A Place at the Table* (*PAT*), the US bishops explain how everyone can assume responsibility for the alleviation of global poverty. They argue that "the Catholic way is to recognize the essential role and the complementary responsibilities of families, communities, the market, and government to work together to overcome poverty and advance human dignity" (*PAT*, no. 34). Using the metaphor of a table, the bishops advocate for the alleviation of poverty and wider participation in decision making. Not only is the table the place where people eat but, as the bishops point out, the table is also where people gather to make decisions and share the Eucharist. The dynamics of globalization have left many of the world's poor without a place at the table—they have insufficient food and they lack a voice in the decisions driving the global economy.

The USCCB suggests that the legs of the table represent entities responsible for preventing and alleviating poverty. The first leg represents individuals and families. The bishops argue against apathy, stating that "every person has a responsibility to respect the dignity

---

14. USCCB, *Catholics Confront Global Poverty*, "The Face of Global Poverty" available at *http://old.usccb.org/sdwp/globalpoverty/pdfs/Backgrounder_The_Face_of_Global_Poverty.pdf.*

of others and to work to secure not only their own rights but also the rights of others" (*PAT*, no. 30). The second leg represents local communities, including churches and faith-based organizations. The bishops note that much work is already being done on local levels by faith communities, such as Catholic schools and hospitals, Catholic Charities, and the Catholic Campaign for Human Development. The bishops remind the reader that "faith is a religious commitment; it is also a community resource" (*PAT*, no. 31).

The USCCB calls on businesses and financial institutions that drive the private sector,[15] the table's third leg, to use their influence on the global market to promote justice for the most vulnerable. The bishops advocate for corporate responsibility, stressing the need for collaboration among employers and the labor movement to ensure just wages and decent working conditions. They express particular concern for people living in poverty, "The process of globalization must provide opportunities for the participation of the poorest people and the economic development of the poorest nations" (*PAT*, no. 32).

Referring to the government as the fourth leg, the US bishops reiterate the Catholic understanding of the positive role of government in protecting the common good. The government, they argue should "provide a safety net for the vulnerable, and help overcome discrimination and ensure equal opportunity for all" (*PAT*, no. 33). Government regulations are particularly important when communities fail to protect the rights of the most vulnerable (*PAT*, no. 33). The bishops emphasize that all four legs have responsibilities to protect human rights. They call on individuals, faith communities, businesses, and governments to collaborate together to overcome challenges to justice that have emerged in the context of globalization.

Reading the Signs of the Times: Globalization and Human Rights

People can ignore the reality of globalization only with great difficulty, and they cannot return to a pre-globalized world. Social ethicist

---

15. The private sector refers to the part of the economy that is not controlled by the state and tends to be driven by for-profit organizations.

Thomas Massaro points out that people cannot reverse the historical process of globalization, but he argues that people can and should try to direct it in a way that promotes justice. Massaro suggests, "It is no longer a matter of *whether* to globalize, but rather *how* to globalize in a way that protects core values as much as possible."[16] This section will explore some of the debates about the nature and ethical dimensions of globalization and, drawing on the work of Catholic social ethicist David Hollenbach, will highlight the challenge of promoting human rights in an interconnected and diverse world.

The Nature and Impact of Economic Globalization

Questions about the nature and ethical implications of economic globalization generate debate. Some for-profit businesses see the potential for global markets to foster development in poor areas and argue that multinational corporations can stimulate the economies of impoverished nations by increasing trade and providing jobs. Critics of globalization, however, note that developing countries tend to lower environmental regulations and labor standards in order to accommodate the wishes of multinational corporations.

The 1999 United Nations World Development Report addressed the problem of the exploitation of the poor by multinational corporations. The UN Development Program argues that globalization can eradicate poverty, but that this potential can be realized only if governing bodies regulate globalization in new ways. Specifically, the UN Development Program calls for stronger forms of governance to protect human rights. The 1999 report states,

> Today's globalization is being driven by market expansion—opening national borders to trade, capital, information—outpacing governance of these markets and their repercussions for people. More progress has been made in norms, standards, policies and institutions for open global markets than for people and their rights.[17]

---

16. Thomas Massaro, *Living Justice: Catholic Social Teaching in Action*, Second Classroom Edition (Lanham, MD: Rowman & Littlefield, 2012), 174.

17. United Nations Development Program Report (1999) "Patterns of Global Inequality" in Held and McGrew, *Global Transformations Reader*, 423.

With all that has been said about globalization, ethicists have cause for great concern and, at the same time, reasons to hope. Social ethicist David Hollenbach suggests that one of the positive aspects of globalization is that it promotes an awareness of shared humanity, the foundation of human rights. He states:

> The human rights ethos conceives of human beings as, first, members of the worldwide human community with rights that derive from their humanity as such and, second, as members of the communities of existing nation states. The globalization of citizenship grants membership in the human community a higher value than citizenship in a particular nation state, at least in extreme situations where humanity itself is threatened.[18]

Hollenbach stresses the need for ongoing dialogue on how to define and promote human rights in a multicultural world. Writing on the context of Africa, Hollenbach suggests that the US notion of human rights is often rejected because it focuses too much on individual freedoms and privacy. One of the problems is that "solidarity with others has little formative role on this individualistic concept of human rights."[19] Hollenbach argues that human rights cannot be construed narrowly as political and civil rights that focus primarily on the protection of individual freedom. To develop a more appropriate and cross-cultural understanding of human rights, individual freedom must be held in relationship to the virtue of solidarity, particularly with the poor. Human rights, especially as seen in developing countries, need to include a strong social dimension, one that touches on people's daily struggles and emphasizes their economic rights.[20]

Hollenbach draws on the Second Vatican Council's approach to human rights to address the modern context. In his reading of *Gaudium et spes*, Hollenbach identifies how rights are framed

---

18. David Hollenbach, "Life in the Global Community," *America* (November 4, 2002): 7.

19. David Hollenbach, *The Global Face of Public Faith: Politics, Human Rights, and Christian Ethics* (Washington, DC: Georgetown University Press, 2003), 220.

20. Ibid., 228.

within the life of a community. The text lists not only basic rights to food and shelter but also to participation in political and economic life—"positive claims to be able to participate actively in the life of the community."[21] Hollenbach makes the point more explicitly, "It was this linkage of the idea of human rights with the common good that enabled the Catholic tradition to see that support for human rights did not require abandonment of the tradition's deep sensitivity to the importance of communal solidarity for human flourishing."[22]

Summary and Integration for Service Learners

This chapter discussed the Catholic Church's advocacy for the rights and responsibilities of the entire human community, especially in relationship to economic globalization. The Catholic social tradition links human rights with responsibilities, a perspective grounded in a commitment to protect the dignity of the individual and promote the common good. Through writings and campaigns, the USCCB has challenged people to take responsibility for protecting the rights of all, especially of the poor throughout the world.

The principle of rights and responsibilities is particularly relevant as the Catholic Church continues to discern the best responses to globalization, one of the signs of the times that invites theological reflection and ethical responses. The globalization of communication makes it possible for people to learn much about human rights violations around the world and also provides opportunities to overcome national and cultural boundaries to create a dialogue on the meaning of human rights and how to protect them.

Revisit your answers to the questions posed at the beginning of this chapter. Would you answer any of them differently? Do you see globalization more as a threat to human rights or as a way to protect human rights throughout the world? Use the following vignette to

---

21. Hollenbach, "Commentary on *Gaudium et Spes*," 281.
22. Ibid.

reflect further on this topic and to practice the see-judge-act process in relation to it.

Working for Fair Trade

Service-Learning Vignette

A service learner decided to work with a national nonprofit organization to promote fair trade products on college campuses because she wanted to advocate for economic rights on an international scale. During her orientation, she learned about the impact of the fair trade system on coffee farmers in Colombia. When farmers are informed about the real value of their product and given resources to market their product to conscientious consumers, they can demand a just wage and employ more sustainable agricultural practices. The student found that most people on her campus were willing to pay more for coffee when they learned about the role of fair trade in protecting people's economic rights.

See: Social Analysis

- What does the vignette reveal about economic globalization? How do the college students willing to buy fair trade coffee relate to the process of globalization? How does the Colombian coffee farmer who receives a just wage relate to globalization?
- What conditions—social, political, economic—contribute to the inequalities that the student is addressing by promoting the purchase of fair trade products?

Judge: Ethical Reflection

- How do you understand the relationship between rights and responsibilities in the Catholic social tradition? How would you apply the principle of rights and responsibilities in assessing the situation of Colombian coffee farmworkers who do not receive fair compensation for their work?
- What is the role of Colombian and US governing bodies, nongovernmental organizations, and individuals in protecting people's economic rights? How might the Catholic social principle of solidarity inform the answers?

Act: Promoting Justice

- Consider what you have learned about human rights and responsibilities from CST and the effects of economic globalization. Identify actions or policies that might ameliorate the negative effects of economic globalization by ensuring the protection of human rights throughout the world.

- Select a local organization, perhaps a service-learning setting, that aims to serve the needs of the poor and consider how the organization's efforts relate to economic globalization. Does the organization try to find solutions to problems caused or exacerbated by such globalization? Does the organization take advantage of opportunities made possible because of economic globalization?

Suggestions for Further Social Analysis in a Service-Learning Context

- Read the United Nations *Universal Declaration of Human Rights*. Using the UN declaration as a guide, investigate whether or not human rights are violated in a service-learning context with which you are familiar.

- Read some perspectives on human rights from different cultural and religious traditions. What are some of the similarities and differences you notice in these perspectives?

- Research the work of multinational nongovernmental organizations that address human rights violations (Amnesty International, Human Rights Watch, etc.). What are some of the issues they address?

For Further Reading on Catholic Social Thought on Globalization and Human Rights

Coleman, John, W. F. Ryan, and Bill Ryan. *Globalization and Catholic Social Thought: Present Crisis, Future Hope.* Maryknoll, NY: Orbis Books, 2005.

Groody, Daniel. *Globalization, Spirituality, and Justice: Navigating the Path to Peace.* Maryknoll, NY: Orbis Press, 2007.

Finn, Daniel, ed. *The Moral Dynamics of Economic Life: An Extension and Critique of* Caritas in Veritate. New York: Oxford University Press, 2012.

Hollenbach, David. *The Common Good and Christian Ethics*. Washington, DC: Georgetown University Press, 2002.

———. *The Global Face of Public Faith: Politics, Human Rights, and Christian Ethics*. Washington, DC: Georgetown University Press, 2003.

APPENDIX

Church Documents Cited

A list of Catholic Church documents cited in the text follows.[1] All Vatican documents can be found at the Vatican's Web site: *www. vatican.va*. All US documents except the two marked with asterisks can be found at the United States Catholic Conference of Bishops' (USCCB) Web site: *www.usccb.org*. The two marked with asterisks are available at *www.old.usccb.org*.

Papal, Conciliar, and Synodal Documents

Pope Benedict XVI, *Caritas in veritate* (*Charity in Truth*), 2009.

Pope John Paul II, *Centesimus annus* (*On the Hundredth Anniversary of* Rerum Novarum), 1991.

Pope John Paul II, *Familiaris consortio* (*On the Role of the Christian Family in the Modern World*) 1981.

Pope John Paul II, *Evangelium vitae* (*The Gospel of Life*), 1981.

Pope John Paul II, *Laborem exercens* (*On Human Work*), 1995.

Pope John Paul II, *Sollicitudo rei socialis* (*On Social Concern*), 1987.

Pope John XXIII, *Mater et magistra* (*Christianity and Social Progress*), 1961.

---

1. A note on gender-inclusive language and church documents: This text aims to use gender-inclusive language whenever possible. However, when quoting church documents, it follows the translation offered by the Vatican or USCCB, which may lack such inclusivity.

Pope John XXIII, *Pacem in terris* (*Peace on Earth*), 1963.

Pope Leo XIII, *Rerum novarum* (*On the Condition of Labor*), 1891.

Pope Paul VI, *Octogesima adveniens* (*A Call to Action*), 1971.

Pope Paul VI, *Populorum progressio* (*The Development of Peoples*), 1967.

Pope Pius XI, *Quadragesimo anno* (*The Reconstruction of Social Order*), 1931.

Pope Pius XII, *Exsul familia Nazarethana* (*The Exiled Family from Nazareth*), 1952.

Second Vatican Council in *Ad gentes* (*Decree on the Missionary Activity of the Church*), 1965.

Second Vatican Council, *Dei verbum* (*Dogmatic Constitution on Divine Revelation*), 1965.

Second Vatican Council, *Gaudium et spes* (*Pastoral Constitution on the Church in the Modern World*), 1965.

Synod of Bishops, *Justice in the World*, 1971.

United States Conference of Catholic Bishops Documents

A Fair and Just Workplace: Principles and Practices, 1999.*

A Place at the Table, 2002.

Brothers and Sisters to Us, Pastoral Letter on Racism, 1979.

Called to Global Solidarity, 1997.

Economic Justice for All, 1986.

"For I Was Hungry and You Gave Me Food:" Catholic Reflections on Food, Farmers, and Farmworkers, 2003.

Forming Consciences for Faithful Citizenship, published before each presidential election since 1999.

Global Climate Change: A Plea for Dialogue, Prudence, and the Common Good, 2001.

Labor Day Statements, published annually since 1986.

Renewing the Earth: An Invitation to Reflection and Action on Environment in Light of Catholic Social Teaching, 1991.

Sharing Catholic Social Teaching: Challenges and Directions, 1997.

Strangers No Longer: Together on a Journey of Hope, A Pastoral Letter Concerning Migration from the Catholic Bishops of Mexico and the United States, 2003.

The Challenge of Peace: God's Promise and Our Response, 1983.*

The Harvest of Justice Is Sown in Peace, 1993.

INDEX

Sidebars and footnotes are referenced with "s" and "n" following the page number.